Thomas Joseph Lawrence

WAR AND NEUTRALITY IN THE FAR EAST

Elibron Classics
www.elibron.com

Elibron Classics series.

ISBN 1-4021-6612-5 (paperback)
ISBN 1-4212-8165-1 (hardcover)

This Elibron Classics Replica Edition is an unabridged facsimile of the edition published in 1904 by Macmillan and Co., Ltd., London and New York.

WAR AND NEUTRALITY
IN THE FAR EAST

WAR AND NEUTRALITY IN THE FAR EAST

BY

T. J. LAWRENCE, M.A., LL.D.

LECTURER IN INTERNATIONAL LAW AT THE ROYAL NAVAL COLLEGE, GREENWICH, AND RECTOR OF UPTON LOVEL, WILTS, ASSOCIATE OF THE INSTITUTE OF INTERNATIONAL LAW, AUTHOR OF 'THE PRINCIPLES OF INTERNATIONAL LAW,' ETC., SOMETIME FELLOW AND TUTOR OF DOWNING COLLEGE, CAMBRIDGE, AND DEPUTY-PROFESSOR OF INTERNATIONAL LAW IN THE UNIVERSITY OF CAMBRIDGE

SECOND EDITION ENLARGED.

London

MACMILLAN AND CO., LIMITED

NEW YORK: THE MACMILLAN COMPANY

1904

First Edition, June 1904
Second Edition, September 1904
Reprinted October 1904

PREFACE TO THE SECOND EDITION

THOUGH a Second Edition of this book appears within three months of the publication of the first, new matter to the extent of nearly seventy pages has been introduced. A fuller consideration of the position of mail-steamers has been rendered indispensable by the seizure of the *Prinz Heinrich.* The exploits of the *Peterburg* and the *Smolensk* made it needful to examine more fully than before the legal status of the Russian Volunteer Fleet, and the international regulations which control the navigation of the Bosphorus and the Dardanelles. The extraordinary trial of the *Allanton,* and the still more extraordinary destruction of the *Knight Commander* without trial, have caused the addition of a new chapter; while the seizure by the Japanese of a Russian destroyer in the harbour of Chifu has necessitated further consideration of the neutrality of China. The inclusion of these and other matters has, I hope, brought the book up to date, and thus increased its usefulness.

It is pleasant to be able to chronicle the acceptance of two views contained in the original text. The correspondent of the *Times* on board the *Haimun* has stated that the use of wireless telegraphy to report the operations of belligerents must be controlled by International Law; and the Prime Minister has declared that belligerent vessels which use the coal obtained in British ports for purposes other than those for which it was granted will not be allowed further supplies.

T. J. LAWRENCE.

UPTON LOVEL RECTORY, WILTS,
September 8, 1904.

PREFACE TO THE FIRST EDITION

THIS little book contains the substance of four lectures given at Cambridge in the Easter Term of the present year, and a paper read at the Royal United Service Institution on May 25. Many of the topics dealt with on these occasions have been amplified, and several questions left untouched then are now carefully considered. On one point only have I seen reason to alter a conclusion previously expressed. At the United Service Institution, while advocating as an object to be kept in view the prohibition of any supplies of coal to belligerent warships in neutral ports, I argued that it would be difficult to propose this and at the same time assert that coal destined for the ordinary purposes of civil life was not contraband of war. Further reflection, and the arguments brought forward in the discussion which followed my paper, have convinced me that the difficulty is more apparent than real. I still hold that total prohibition, though eminently desirable in itself, is impossible for the present; but the supposed inconsistency of advocating it and also maintaining that coal is not always contraband vanishes when we consider that the supreme importance of a commodity for warlike purposes does not make it less supremely important for domestic uses. The need of coal for both can hardly be exaggerated; and therefore it is advisable that neutrals should not permit combatant vessels to be supplied with it in their ports, while belligerents should not attempt to stop a neutral trade in it for the purpose of satisfying the wants of the ordinary civilian population of the enemy's country.

My thanks are due, and are hereby tendered, to several friends for valuable aid. Without the advice and encouragement of Dr. C. S. Kenny, Reader in English Law in the University of Cambridge, the lectures at Cambridge would never have been given, and this book would never have been written. Captain E. J. W. Slade, R.N., M.V.O., Captain of the Royal Naval College, Greenwich, has most kindly supplied me with information at a time when the pressure of his own work was very heavy upon him. I have felt at every turn the advantage of many a long discussion with Captain A. A. C. Galloway, R.N., now in command of the *Revenge*, on the problems of International Law raised by the changed conditions of modern warfare and modern commerce. Miss E. P. Hughes has ungrudgingly given me the fruit of the experience gained in her educational mission to Japan, and her knowledge of the inner life of the Japanese people. Had Rear-Admiral H. J. May been still alive, I should have rejoiced to convey to him my grateful acknowledgments of pregnant hints and subtle suggestions. Unfortunately it is not possible to do more than pay a tribute to his memory. I hope no landsman's misapprehensions have impaired the value of what I have received from naval friends. If it be so, let me exonerate them from all blame. The accuracies are theirs; the mistakes are my own. Yet I trust the book, with all its faults, will help a little towards the formation of sound opinion on important matters of public policy. Judging by what one hears and reads, there is often need of guidance. I have striven to write from the point of view of a student of international affairs, without bias and without partiality. If I have a predilection, it is an excusable one for my own country and its interests.

In a work based largely on the facts reported in the newspapers from day to day, it seemed out of place to print references, which must have been inconveniently numerous if they were given at all. The principles of International Law laid down are the common property of jurists, though some of the applications of them are my own. I have referred in the text to a few great authorities; and I cannot conclude without acknowledging the help I derived in writing the historical parts of the book from a series of articles on the Manchurian Question which appeared in the *Times* during the first weeks of the present year.

T. J. LAWRENCE.

UPTON LOVEL RECTORY, WILTS,
June 16, 1904.

CONTENTS

CHAPTER I

CHAPTER II

CHAPTER III

CHAPTER IV

CHAPTER V

CHAPTER VI

CHAPTER VII

CHAPTER VIII

CHAPTER IX

CHAPTER X

CHAPTER XI

CHAPTER I

THE QUARREL

In order to discover the causes of the present conflict between Russia and Japan, we must go back for ten years, and dwell for a moment on the late war between Japan and China. Then, as now, the main grounds of quarrel centred in Korea. Then, as now, the statesmen of Tokio objected strongly to any foreign influence within the borders of the Hermit Kingdom. Then, as now, they established their own authority at the Court of Seoul, and used it to direct policy as well as reform administration. And the reason on both occasions was the same. It is a matter of life and death for Japan to keep Korea out of the hands of any strong and aggressive State.

She can no more afford to let it fall under the domination of Russia, or even of China, than Great Britain can afford to let Ireland belong to France or Germany. Dublin is eighty-four miles from Holyhead. Less than double that distance separates Fusan from Shimonoseki, or Masampo from Sasebo. A glance at the map is sufficient to show that a powerful empire entrenched in South-eastern Korea would be a perpetual menace to the independence of Japan. Moreover, the Japanese people have grown to such numbers that they need an outlet beyond the sea, and cannot resign into strong hands their nearest field for colonisation and expansion. It is true that only fifteen per cent of the three large islands is cultivated; but the best authorities declare that, owing to the nature of the soil and the abundance of mountains and lakes, no more can be utilised, except, perhaps, a few thousand acres in the northern island of Hokkaido. What can be worked is tilled like a garden. Yet the utmost skill and industry will not provide food for more than fifty millions of people, whereas the population is rapidly increasing, and will soon pass that limit. The inevitable overspill into neighbouring lands has already begun; and it is of the utmost importance that the rulers of the country most favourably situated for Japanese immigration shall be prepared to welcome it.

These considerations will help to explain the extreme anxiety felt in Japan with regard to the political future of Korea. It is the fate of peninsula-states to exercise a vast influence upon their neighbours. If they are strong, they dominate the regions on either side of them; if they are weak, they are themselves dominated. The latter has been the lot of the Korean Empire. For centuries it has been a battle-ground whereon China and Japan contended for mastery. In 1860 a third power appeared on the distant horizon. Russia acquired the maritime province of Siberia by cession from China, and thus brought her Asiatic frontier down to the river Tumen, where for eleven miles it bordered on Korean territory. For a time she rested to consolidate her gains; and meanwhile the relations between China and Japan grew steadily worse. The former power looked upon the latter as a renegade from the cause of Oriental seclusion, and a pervert to the grasping, mechanical Western civilisation, which she accounted the most noxious form of barbarism. And this feeling was all the stronger because it was from China that Japan had obtained her art, her writing, her ancient education, two of her religions, and her philosophy. Japan retorted with scorn for the antiquated methods and unbending conservatism of her huge rival. The two chief Empires of the Far East grew more and more divided in sympathy every day; and while they bickered, the smaller and weaker Empire of Korea sank deeper and deeper in the mire of intrigue and corruption, till its Government became a byword even among Oriental peoples.

A curious result of the helplessness of Korea had been that from time immemorial she had placed herself in a position of dependence towards both of her great neighbours. Whether as three kingdoms or as one, she was the victim of internal dissensions and the prey of foreign conquerors. In the latter half of the fourteenth century, the first of the present ruling family, a successful soldier named Litan, voluntarily placed his country under the suzerainty of Hong Wou, the great founder of the Ming Dynasty in China. Two hundred years afterwards Hideyoshi, the Napoleon of Japan, sent a large army to invade Korea. China came to the rescue; and for six years a most cruel and destructive warfare was carried on with doubtful results. The balance of victory inclined towards the Japanese side on land and the Chinese at sea. The unfortunate Koreans found themselves between the hammer and the anvil, and suffered terribly from both. Much of the present hopeless condition of the people can be traced to the horrors of the great invasion. This fact explains both their indifference to political and social reform, and their special objection to Japan as the instrument of either. It also acts as an incentive to some of the best of the Japanese people, in their efforts to make up for past wrongs by bringing about a present regeneration, according to the methods which have proved so successful among themselves.

Hideyoshi died in 1598, and on his death-bed ordered the recall of the Japanese troops from Korea. They returned, having obtained for their countrymen somewhat greater privileges than before in the port of Fusan, and for their country a heavy tribute from the Korean kingdom. But the gains were altogether disproportionate to the effort; and Korea sank back into an indeterminate position of political subservience, first to one and then to the other of the neighbouring Empires. The Chinese claim of an ill-defined superiority was always kept up. But it became the policy of Japan, after her own great awakening in 1868, to insist upon Korean independence. Independence, however, was to be understood in a decidedly Pickwickian fashion. The constant interventions of China were to come to an end, and her influence was no longer to be exerted in favour of the old corrupt system of government. At the same time the country was to be reformed under Japanese tutelage by the introduction of Westernised methods. In 1876, as a punishment for an attack upon a coast-surveying party, Japan sent over a fleet and forced upon the Hermit Kingdom a treaty of amity and commerce. Its first Article declared Korea to be "an independent state enjoying the same rights as Japan," and it went on to open three Korean ports to foreign trade. Within the next few years the leading Powers of Europe and the United States of America negotiated commercial treaties with the Court of Seoul, as with an independent government, without any protest from Peking. Yet, as regards Japan and her attempts at reform, the claim of suzerainty was kept up, often with the most irritating results, as when in 1882, and again in 1884, after Chinese intervention against the reformers, the Japanese legation in Seoul was attacked and burned. After the first of these outbreaks Japan obtained by treaty a right to maintain troops in Seoul for the protection of her diplomatic minister, and after the second she entered into an agreement with China whereby each power promised not to send armed forces into Korea without informing the other of the despatch of the expedition.

There would be little profit in a minute

account of the events which immediately preceded the outbreak of war between China and Japan in July 1894. It was the old story over again of Korean exclusiveness and corruption, bolstered up by Chinese aid, and Japanese determination to rule out other influences and assert her own, by insisting upon reform. There was the usual insurrection against the effete native Government, the usual intervention of China to put it down, followed on this occasion by the unusual despatch of a Japanese force to watch and check that of the intervening Empire. In the negotiations which followed, China persisted in describing Korea as her "tributary State," while Japan declared that she was an independent power. The proposal of the latter for joint action in reforming the peninsula-empire was scouted. The statesmen of Tokio declared in reply that they would undertake the work themselves, and warned China that any attempt to reinforce her troops in Korea would be regarded as an act of hostility. In spite of this notification, fresh forces were sent, with the result that hostilities commenced on July 25.

On the same day, the royal palace at Seoul having been previously occupied by Japanese troops, the diplomatic representative of Japan obtained from the overawed Emperor a commission to expel the intruding Chinese soldiers from his territory. This was followed in August by a treaty of alliance, the main object of which, as stated in its first Article, was "to maintain the independence of Korea on a firm footing."

Everybody knows the result of the war. Japan astonished the world by the completeness of her preparations and the skill with which her forces were handled. After an uninterrupted series of victories by land and sea, she dictated the terms of peace. The first Article of the Treaty of Shimonoseki, signed in April and ratified on May 8, 1895, ran thus:—

"China recognises definitely the full and complete independence and autonomy of Korea, and in consequence the payment of tribute and the performance of ceremonies and formalities by Korea to China, in derogation of such independence and autonomy, shall wholly cease for the future."

By the next Article various territorial cessions were provided for. In addition to Formosa and a number of other islands, China was to make over to Japan in full sovereignty the fortress of Port Arthur, which had been captured by a Japanese army during the war, and the Liau-tung peninsula, at the end of which Port Arthur stands.

Scarcely was the ink of the treaty dry when startling action was taken by the great world-power which had in 1860 obtained a frontier just touching the north-east corner of Korean territory. Since that time Russia had greatly developed her Asiatic provinces. She had also created a strongly-fortified harbour in the south of her newly-won territory, and this she called by the proud name of Vladivostock, "The Empire of the East." It was to be the terminus of the marvellous line of railway, commenced in 1891, which traverses two continents for a distance of 6000 miles, and links the Baltic Sea with the Pacific Ocean. But its waters are frozen for some months in the year, and the need of an ice-free port at the end of so great an artery of communication as the Siberian Railway forced Russian statesmen to seek farther south for an outlet to the sea. Japan at Port Arthur stood in their way, and, backed by France and Germany, they determined to oust her. On April 25, 1895, the following note was presented to the Government of Tokio:—

"The Imperial Russian Government, having examined the terms of peace demanded of China by Japan, consider the contemplated possession of the Liau-tung peninsula by Japan will not only constitute a constant menace to the capital of China, but will also render the independence of Korea illusory, and thus jeopardise the permanent peace of the Far East. Accordingly, the Imperial Government, in a spirit of cordial friendship for Japan, hereby counsel the Government of the Emperor of Japan to renounce the definitive possession of the Liau-tung peninsula."

It was well known that the courteous phraseology of this note concealed a determination on the part of the three powers to enforce its recommendations. Japan was in no condition to defy them; and accordingly the Emperor published along with the ratified treaty an Imperial Rescript, in which he "yielded to the dictates of magnanimity, and accepted the advice of the three powers." But the pill was none the less bitter because it was swallowed with a smile; and from that time onwards a feeling of keen resentment against Russia filled the minds of the Japanese people, who were still further embittered by the failure of an attempt to obtain from China an undertaking that she would never cede to a third power the restored territory.

The prescience of their statesmen in asking for this pledge was justified in 1898. In that year Germany obtained from China a ninety-nine years' lease of Kiao-Chau Bay and the adjacent territory, and Russia immediately exacted a similar concession. Port Arthur and Ta-lien-wan, now Dalny, with the adjacent territories and territorial waters, were "ceded in usufruct" to her for twenty-five years, with a power of extension by common accord. She further received permission to carry her Manchurian railway down to Port Arthur through Chinese territory. Japan had, therefore, the mortification of seeing the prize of which she had been deprived appropriated by the power which had taken the lead in the act of deprivation. One of the pretexts put forward to justify her expulsion had been that the possession of the Liau-tung peninsula by a strong power would menace Korean independence. The conduct of Russia soon showed the cogency of her own arguments; for early in 1900 she attempted to get a grip on Masampo, the Gibraltar of Korea; and if she had succeeded in fortifying a position there, she would have had a strong naval base within a few hours' steam of important Japanese ports.

But though Japan had retired at the moment, it was only in order to prepare for a future advance. The navy, which has recently given such a splendid account of itself at Port Arthur, is a creation of the last nine years. The squadron which won the battle of the Yalu in 1895 was made up of cruisers; and among its eleven vessels there was none much larger than 5000 tons. The fleet which now dominates the Korean Bay and the Gulf of Liau-tung contains five magnificent battleships, the biggest of which has nearly three times the tonnage, and much more than three times the fighting power, of the most formidable of the victors in the earlier struggle. The army, too, has been more than doubled. About 120,000 men brought China to her knees a decade ago. At the present moment more than 500,000 can be summoned to fight beneath the Sun Flag.

But though Japan assiduously prepared for war, and endeavoured by careful diplomacy to recover the position in Korea she had lost in consequence of her rebuff in 1895 and the influence gained at Seoul by the able Russian minister, M. Pavloff, it is quite possible there would have been no war between her and Russia, but for events which occurred in Manchuria. The most experienced Japanese statesmen saw clearly the terrible hazards of a conflict, and the disastrous consequences of failure. They would have preferred to gain something by agreement, rather than risk the loss of all by war. But every effort in this direction failed; and the Boxer outbreak in China in the summer of 1900 added fresh causes of quarrel to those already in existence. While the fate of the foreign legations at Peking was trembling in the balance, the Chinese authorities in Manchuria attacked the Russian officials and settlers. Russia promptly moved large forces into the province, and exacted a terrible retribution. At Blagovestchensk the Amur River was blocked with 5000 Chinese corpses, and similar scenes on a lesser scale were enacted in other places. In a few weeks the whole province was in Russian military occupation. These operations were described in a diplomatic circular issued on August 25, 1900, as "exclusively prompted by the necessity of warding off the aggressive acts of the Chinese rebels," and the assurance was given that—

"As soon as lasting order shall have been established in Manchuria, and indispensable measures shall have been taken for the protection of the railway . . . Russia will not fail to recall her troops from these territories of the neighbouring Empire, provided that the action of the other powers does not place any obstacle in the way of such a measure."

This was but the first of a long series of similar statements, which, however, harmonised ill with the continued presence of Russian troops, the enormous concessions demanded from China as the price of the restoration to her of the civil administration of the province, and the incessant attempt to deprive other powers of the commercial privileges they enjoyed as a matter of treaty-right. It is to be noted, too, that this assurance, and the others that followed it, contained saving clauses of ingenious wording and elastic purport. Who was to judge when "lasting order" was established, and what measures were "indispensable" for the protection of the railway? How was it to be settled whether the action of the "other powers" did or did not place any "obstacle" in the way of evacuation?

There would be little profit in running through the list of carefully-guarded pledges, even if the task were as pleasant as it is repulsive. But it is necessary to allude to one of them, because it took the form of a solemn international agreement, which would probably have prevented the present war, had it been properly fulfilled. I refer to the Manchurian Convention between Russia and China, of April 8, 1902. By its second Article China undertook to observe strictly the terms of her contract of 1896 with the Russo-Chinese Bank concerning the Manchurian Railway; and in consideration of this Russia covenanted—

"In the event of there being no trouble whatsoever, and if the conduct of other powers should not interpose any obstacle thereto, to withdraw gradually all Russian troops from Manchuria."

The Article went on to state that the south-western portion of the province, up to the Liao River, was to be evacuated within six months of the signature of the Convention. Six months after that another district was to be restored to China, and during the next six months the remaining part. By October 8, 1902, Russia withdrew from the first of these three zones, though even here the evacuation amounted to little more than moving the Russian troops from their camps and garrisons to points on the Manchurian Railway, where they acted as guards.

When the turn of the second zone came on April 8, 1903, the evacuation was "temporarily delayed." The delay has continued up to the present moment; and no attempt has been made to carry out the promise, which fell due on the 8th of last October, to give up the third zone by that date. Instead, assurances were freely tendered that the treaty-rights enjoyed by other powers in the districts in question would be recognised; and the blame of the non-fulfilment of the Convention of April 1902 was thrown upon China. It is by conduct such as this, joined with persistent endeavours to establish a Russian trade monopoly in every district under Russian influence, that the great Northern Empire has alienated sympathy, especially in England and America, and turned men's minds towards her Eastern rival, who is the champion of equal commercial opportunities for all.

Meanwhile a keen diplomatic conflict was going on between Russia and Japan at the Court of Seoul, where the former power played the part taken by China in the period before the war of

1894. The weapons employed were intrigue, bribery, and even assassination. In 1895 the Queen was murdered in the palace by the Japanese faction, and the King made prisoner. After some months he escaped, and took refuge in the Russian legation, where he remained for more than a year. During this period the reforms due to the action of Japan were dropped, and the old abuses revived—a retrograde step for which the assumption by the King of the title of Emperor in 1897 can hardly be regarded as sufficient compensation. Russia continually showed by her acts that she did not mean her power and influence to stop short at the south-western border of Manchuria. We have already (see p. 13) alluded to her attempt to obtain a lease of Masampo in 1900. On its failure, she tried to gain possession of a naval station in the neighbouring bay of Ching-kai-wan. Unsuccessful here, she turned her attention to Northern Korea. A concession to cut timber on the Yalu and Tumen rivers had been obtained in 1896, and was renewed in 1903. In the latter year a right to construct telegraphs and railways, and even fortifications, was read into it. There could be little doubt that the Korean side of the lower Yalu was marked down for Russian settlement; and experience shows that Russian settlement means much the same thing as Russian rule. Japan could not but regard such an extension of her great neighbour's territory as a danger to herself. She made vigorous protests; and at last, in the summer of 1903, opened direct negotiations with the Government of St. Petersburg in the hope of reaching a satisfactory agreement.

Until we have access to all the papers connected with these negotiations, it is impossible to speak with absolute certainty of the course they took. But from the justificatory communications published by Russia and Japan at the outbreak of the war, and the despatches since made public, it seems clear that

(*a*) Both Powers were willing to recognise in words the independence and territorial integrity of Korea, but they interpreted the phrase differently. Japan claimed the right to send troops into the country in order to protect her interests in the event of disturbances, and also desired to be free to occupy Korean territory for strategic purposes. To this last proposal Russia refused to agree, and on her part suggested that the northern portion of Korea should be made into a neutral zone. Japan would not hear of this unless a district on the Manchurian side of the border were neutralised also, and declined to pledge herself to refrain from the use of Korean territory for strategic purposes.

(*b*) Japan proposed a mutual engagement to respect the independence and territorial integrity of China, and maintain the principle of equal opportunity for the commerce and industry of all nations in Chinese territory. Russia offered instead a declaration to foreign cabinets that as long as her occupation of Manchuria lasted she would recognise Chinese sovereignty therein, and also the privileges acquired by the powers through their treaties with China. Not only did she refuse to include Manchurian affairs in the proposed treaty with Japan, but she required the latter power to recognise that Manchuria was outside the sphere of her interests.

The negotiations dragged on for more than six months, during which both parties made extensive preparations for war. At last, on February 6, 1904, Japan, tired of Russian delays, and moved to anger by the departure of the squadron of Admiral Wirenius from Suez for the Far East, broke off diplomatic intercourse with her great rival. Before we turn to the consideration of some of the points of International Law that have arisen with reference to the contest, let us consider for a moment the position, diplomatic and actual, of the two powers, and glance at the issues at stake.

There is an air of unreality about all the asseverations with regard to the integrity and independence of Korea. For ten years Russia and Japan have been rivals for influence over that country. Korea, too weak and too corrupt to protect herself, has been swayed alternately by one and the other of the neighbouring Empires. She cannot stand alone. The real question is, which shall prop her up, and prop her up in its own interest rather than in hers. Japan controlled her in the war with China.

Japan controls her now, and by the recent treaty of February 27 has assumed what amounts to a protectorate over her. If Japan is successful in the present war, she will remain a protecting power, under whatever diplomatic forms the fact may be disguised. If she fails, Russia will take her place. I have no doubt that in the long run Korea will be annexed by one or the other of her powerful neighbours. It is the fate of small, weak, and corrupt states to fade out of the political map; and no one need shed sentimental tears over the disappearance of an independence so shamefully misused as has been that of the Hermit Kingdom. But we may be allowed to hope that, if the Japanese receive her as the prize of victory, they will develop an aptitude for governing subordinate peoples which history shows to have been wanting to them in the past.

With regard to Manchuria, Russia's protestations of respect for Chinese sovereignty deceive no one, least of all the astute statesmen who utter them in the Czar's name. The victory of Russia in the present struggle means the addition of that province to her Empire, and probably the destruction in consequence of all the commercial and industrial privileges enjoyed in it by foreign nations under their treaties with China. The precedent of Madagascar would no doubt be followed. There Russia's ally, France, on adding the country to her colonial dominions in 1896, applied her own tariff to foreign trade, and set aside the commercial privileges secured to British and American citizens by previous treaties with the native Hova Government. This gave rise to a diplomatic correspondence of no very friendly kind; and one of the conditions of the recent happy accord between the two powers was that our Government should renounce the protest it made at the time. On the other hand, if the war ends in favour of Japan, she will restore Manchuria to China in full sovereignty, but will doubtless claim some reward from the gratitude of the Government of Peking. The policy of the "open door" will be followed in commercial matters; but in all probability, to use a fashionable diplomatic phrase, the "political permeation" of China by Japan will be undertaken on a large scale.

The story we have told is not particularly edifying. The causes of the war can be traced: its consequences no one can pretend to foresee. Here and there glimpses of a probable future may be obtained, and they present a curious mixture of good and evil. Those who fear "the yellow peril," and regard Russia as the great bulwark against it, will ardently desire the triumph of the Czar's arms. But those who believe that the Japanese are destined to become the connecting-link between East and West, by interpreting what is best in the mind of each to the other, and thus bringing them together peacefully instead of arraying them in mortal conflict, will wish the island-Empire well in its efforts to roll back a danger which threatens its position as an important power, if not its national existence.

CHAPTER II

THE OUTBREAK OF WAR AND THE LAWS OF WAR. WAS JAPAN TREACHEROUS?

JAPAN broke off diplomatic relations with Russia on February 6, 1904. Towards midnight on February 8, her torpedo-boats dashed into the harbour of Port Arthur, and wrought terrible havoc among the vessels of the Russian Pacific squadron. Earlier in the day a shot or two had been fired, possibly by accident, outside the harbour of Chemulpo, and a Japanese squadron had landed troops in the place. But nothing of sufficient consequence to be called an engagement took place, before the attack on the Russian fleet as it lay in the outer roadstead of the great naval port at the point of the Liau-tung peninsula. Japan followed up her blow by a declaration of war, which, however, was not issued till February 10. On the same day the Czar, when granting commissions to naval ensigns, took the opportunity to denounce Japan as a treacherous foe. The charge was repeated in his manifesto published in the *Official Messenger* of that date, and in the Circular sent on February 22 by Count Lamsdorff, his Minister for Foreign Affairs, to the Russian diplomatic representatives abroad. Thus fathered, it received attention throughout the civilised world. Many French and German papers took it up eagerly; and though in English-speaking countries it did not meet with much acceptance, it gave considerable uneasiness to sympathisers with Japan. It will be desirable, therefore, to examine it with some care.

The accusation of treachery rests entirely upon the assumption that International Law imposes upon belligerents the duty of making to one another a formal declaration of war before commencing hostilities. Never was assumption more groundless. Nearly every war of the last two centuries has been commenced without a declaration. Sometimes one has been issued, as in the present case, a greater or less time after the forces of the combatants have begun their work of conflict. Sometimes there has been none from the beginning to the end of a war. Occasionally a manifesto by a State to its own subjects, or a diplomatic circular sent to foreign Governments, has taken the place of formal notice delivered to the enemy. The constant practice has been for the better-prepared state to strike a sudden blow at her unready adversary, whatever form or absence of form seemed advisable at the moment. Nor is there in this anything that necessarily involves bad faith. A period of negotiation precedes a period of hostility. As relations grow more and more strained, a prudent state prepares for eventualities. Very often an *ultimatum* is presented, that is to say, a demand the refusal of which will be followed by war. The rupture of diplomatic relations is the constant precursor of armed conflict. Unless the first blow falls, like a bolt from the blue, in a period of profound peace, without previous complaint and demand for redress, there is nothing in it which savours of treachery. Yet so rooted is the notion, derived from the ages of chivalry, of the unfairness of an attack on an enemy without giving him notice beforehand, that the commencement of an undeclared war is constantly mourned over as a sad example of lawlessness and perfidy. Yet even in the days of chivalry the formal notice often initiated a struggle for which there were no reasons beyond ambition or greed, and sometimes it was purposely contrived to convey an insult, as when Charles V. of France sent his challenge to Edward III. of England in 1369 by the hand of a kitchen-servant.

As an example of the practice of modern times we will quote two instances, one from the recent history of each of the parties to the present war. In May 1853, a Russian army entered what were then the Turkish provinces of Moldavia and Wallachia, and occupied them as a "material guarantee" for the maintenance of the rights of the Greek Christians in the Ottoman Empire. This was clearly an act of hostility, though Russia loudly declared it to be nothing of the kind. But no declaration of war followed till Turkey made one in the following October. The first engagement of the war of a decade ago between Japan and China was fought in Korean waters on July 25, 1894. The formal declaration of war by the Emperor of Japan was dated August 1. Yet we find Count Ito, Minister President of State, writing officially on September 10, 1894, "Let it be known that the commencement of the present war was the 25th of July." What was done on these two occasions, first by one and then by the other of the present belligerents, has been done habitually by civilised powers. General Maurice proves this to demonstration in his monograph on *Hostilities without Declaration of War*, published in 1883; and in an article in the *Nineteenth Century and After* for the month of April, 1904, he sums up his results in the following words, which refer to attacks without declaration:—

"Numerically, within the time I more particularly examined, Britain struck thirty of these blows, France thirty-six, Russia seven (not reckoning her habitual practice towards Turkey and other bordering Asiatic States, including China), Prussia seven, Austria twelve, the United States five at least."

Unless, therefore, we are prepared to maintain the ridiculous proposition that the law of nations, instead of being deduced from the practice of nations, has no connection whatever with it, we must acquit Japan of the charge made against her. Instead of being guilty of a violation of International Law, she went beyond it by giving her adversary ample notice of what he might expect. Relations between the two Powers had been strained for a long time. There would have been no treachery in a sudden attack. But the Note delivered on February 6 by the Japanese Representative at St. Petersburg not only broke off diplomatic intercourse—an act which is constantly followed by immediate war—but also expressly stated that Japan must take such measures as she thought fit for her own safety. Its exact words were, "The Imperial Government reserve to themselves the right to take such independent action as they may deem best to consolidate and defend their menaced position, as well as to protect their established rights and legitimate interests." The merest tyro in diplomacy knows what this meant. It was a distinct warning that hostilities might be expected at any moment, and the first blow was not struck till about sixty hours after it had been given. As a matter of fact, Russia was not taken unawares. She had expected war for some time, and had prepared for it, though her preparations were ill conceived and badly carried out. In this connection a significant interview with Captain Stepanoff of the *Variag* appeared early in April in the *Neues Wiener Tagblatt.* I quote it, as translated in the *Standard* of April 7, merely reminding those who read it that the *Variag* was the famous Russian cruiser which fought a Japanese squadron for an hour outside Chemulpo on February 9, 1904, and was scuttled afterwards by her own crew (see pp. 67-69). The captain's words are,

"For months, so to say, we had expected every moment the breaking off of diplomatic relations, and we knew that war with Japan was inevitable. Our squadron was preparing in all earnestness, and day and night work went on, as we were awaiting a declaration of war by Japan every hour."

These sentences show that some at least of the Czar's officers were able to read the signs of the times, and energetic enough to act on them. But foresight was not a monopoly of the naval service. The Russian Government steadily strengthened its forces in the Far East during the six months that preceded the outbreak of hostilities. Indeed, the despatch of its squadron from the port of Suez on February 4 was in all probability the determining event which caused the rulers of Japan to decide in favour of immediate war. There is some reason to suppose that the northern border of Korea was crossed by reconnoitring Cossacks while the two Empires were still at peace. Even in Port Arthur, the home of overweening confidence, there were preparations. On February 3 the Russian squadron therein, reinforced by ships of the "Armed Reserve," put out to sea, possibly to practise evolutions in view of hostilities, possibly to look out for a Japanese force. The fact that five days afterwards, when the attack was at last delivered, the officers were engaged in festivity, proves them negligent, but does not prove their foes treacherous. Russia's charge against Japan deserves no serious consideration. It is merely an attempt to conceal her own deficiencies by imputing bad faith to an honourable enemy.

It may be advisable to explain here what is meant when we speak of the parties to a war as being bound to observe certain rules in their dealings with each other and with neutrals. Civilised belligerents come under the somewhat elastic code which goes by the name of the Laws of War. It is founded on the practices and agreements of enlightened states, and with regard to many of its provisions is as clear and certain as the law of the land. This is specially the case when the rules in question apply universally accepted principles of enlightened morality. There is no doubt, for instance, that it is unlawful to slaughter prisoners, or sink neutral vessels engaged in innocent commerce, or fire on a flag of truce, or let loose troops to plunder and outrage helpless non-combatants.

Moreover, every self-respecting state will take care to observe any agreements to which it has set its signature, even when they impose obligations of a technical character unconnected with justice or humanity, such, for example, as an arrangement for the exchange of prisoners. But outside these matters of certainty there are others as to which we find differences of opinion and divergences in action. The law of blockade supplies an illustration. France holds that the master of every blockade-runner is entitled to individual and direct notice of the existence of the blockade he seeks to violate, while we maintain that a diplomatic notification to neutral Governments is sufficient in all but exceptional cases. Where practice is uniform, or the matter is provided for by express agreement, the rule is clear. Failing one or the other of these two conditions, there is room for doubt and difficulty. In the present conflict both belligerents are, of course, bound by the ordinary rules of warfare. One of them has gone out of her way to enumerate the recent international agreements to which she considers herself under obligation to conform, in addition to those whose provisions she has expressly embodied in her published regulations. The document which does this is the Order of the Czar of February 28, 1904. It is entitled

Rules which the Imperial Government will enforce during the War with Japan

Many of its statements are very important, and we shall often have to refer to it. The tenth Article declares that the military authorities are bound to observe—

The Geneva Convention of 1864, which neutralises, that is to say, exempts from the operations of warlike force, persons and things connected with the care of the sick and wounded in warfare on land.

The Declaration of St. Petersburg of 1868, which prohibits the use of explosive bullets.

The Convention with respect to the laws and customs of warfare on land, negotiated at the Hague Conference of 1899.

The Convention, also negotiated at the Hague Conference, for adapting to maritime warfare the principles of the Geneva Convention.

The three Declarations agreed to by most of the

States represented at the Hague Conference—the *first* prohibiting for five years the use of projectiles dropped from balloons, the *second* prohibiting the use of projectiles which are only intended to spread asphyxiating or noxious fumes, and the *third* prohibiting the use of bullets which expand and flatten easily in the human body.

Japan is no less bound than Russia by these international agreements. She has signed them all, and has hitherto given the world no reason to suppose that her signature will not be honoured. Still, the special enumeration of them in the Russian "Rules" is significant, and affords another proof of the desire of the sorely-tried Czar to lessen the horrors of warfare.

It is difficult to obtain full and unprejudiced information about the events of the struggle. But the facts before us up to the present time, always excepting the wolfish ferocity reported from Port Arthur in August and September, justify on the whole a favourable judgment of the behaviour of the combatants to each other. The customary complaints have not been altogether absent, particularly on the part of Russia.

We must remember, in considering what weight to attach to them, that sometimes the pen is employed against an opponent as actively as the sword, especially when it is important to divert sympathy from one side to the other. The first and most important of these accusations we have already found to be baseless. Others will be dealt with in due time. But another and probably more important group of questions arises with regard to the relations between belligerents and neutrals. The war has already yielded a heavy crop of these problems, the chief of which will be presented in the following pages. Before passing on to their consideration it will be advisable to dismiss in a few words two or three matters closely connected with the humanities of warfare.

At the commencement of the conflict there was a rush of Japanese fugitives seeking to return to their country from Manchuria and the Russian dominions in Eastern Asia. On February 18 the Japanese Legation in London issued, in the form of a diary, a moving narrative of the sufferings of a number of their compatriots who attempted to leave Port Arthur. According to this account they were robbed, detained for days on board the steamers on which they had embarked, left without food and drink, and reduced to a pitiable condition before they were allowed to depart. These stories of brutality received a certain amount of corroboration from other sources, and were certainly not refuted by the counter-allegation that the Japanese thus maltreated were of bad character. On the other hand, much of the cruelty complained of seems to have been due to the action of the mob and lawless subordinate officials. Admiral Alexeieff, the Czar's Viceroy in the Far East, exerted himself to secure better treatment of the refugees; and after a time the barbarities ceased. Some of the later bands of returning fugitives spoke with thankfulness of the kindness they received. It is clear that an unwieldy and ill-organised administration, suddenly exposed to the strain of a great war, broke down in this matter as in most others, and was unable at first to restrain the worst instincts of its own people. Afterwards, as order was slowly evolved from chaos, subjects of the enemy shared the benefits of the general improvement.

The sinking of a number of Japanese vessels by the Russian Vladivostock squadron is another matter which provoked much unfavourable comment. The first case occurred on February 11, when the *Nakonoura Maru* was surrounded and destroyed. The first accounts implied that all on board had been sent to the bottom along with her. Had they been true, a gross outrage would have been committed. A belligerent cruiser has a right to stop, search, and seize any merchantman of the enemy it may meet outside neutral waters. But it has no right to destroy, unless its summons to surrender is disregarded, or its search resisted, or an attempt made to recapture the vessel or to escape after surrender. It may then use force to attain its proper end of capture, and if incidentally the ship is sunk, her crew have only themselves to thank. But to send helpless mariners to their death without giving them an opportunity of surrender would be an act of cruel and lawless violence. Fortunately for the credit of Russian humanity, no such iniquity was committed. Further information showed that the crew of the *Nakonoura Maru* were taken on board a Russian man-of-war and conveyed to Vladivostock, from whence they were sent back to Japan by a German steamer. Clearly, they received from their captors all proper treatment. A legal purist might perhaps blame the Russian commander for sinking his prize at sea, instead of taking her before a Prize Court for adjudication. But when we remember that the weather at the time was terrific, and the ship unseaworthy owing to the damage it had received, we shall not attach much weight to such a judgment. No neutral rights were involved. It was an enemy vessel; and between enemies superior force prevails to destroy proprietary rights. A trial before a Prize Court would have been advisable, if it had been reasonably possible; but there are good grounds for believing that it was not.

The same considerations apply to the case of the trading steamer *Goyo Maru*, except that the reason for not sending her in for adjudication by a Prize Court was the close proximity of a superior Japanese squadron. She was sunk on April 25 in the Bay of Gensan, after her crew of twenty men had been put in a boat and told to make for land. The case of the *Kinshiu Maru*, which occurred a few hours afterwards, was a still stronger one from the Russian point of view. She was a Japanese transport, carrying troops and coals. Mistaking in the fog which prevailed the Russian cruisers for her own, she went towards them signalling, "I am bringing you coal." A summons to surrender revealed her mistake. Some of the troops on board made a most heroic but hopeless resistance. The rest appear to have surrendered, and were taken on board the Russian vessels as prisoners of war. In the end the transport was sunk by means of a torpedo, and her brave defenders went to the bottom along with her, continuing to fire as the waves closed over them. Their resistance evokes our warm admiration, but it amply justified their enemies in destroying them and their ship.

There will be no need to consider at any

length the charge against the Japanese of firing upon a Red Cross train running out of Port Arthur on May 6, when they were effecting their first landing upon the Liau-tung peninsula. The answer to it is very simple. The train was not devoted entirely to the service of the sick and wounded. Several compartments were filled with them; but either the Red Cross badge was not displayed or the Japanese did not see it. The rest of the train contained women and children, and combatant officers. Indeed, according to some accounts, Admiral Alexeieff was in it. The Japanese assert that some of the Russian soldiers in the train fired at them and they responded. Whereupon the engine halted, and a Red Cross flag was hoisted. They then ceased to fire, and endeavoured to ascertain whether the vehicles in front of them were under the protection of the Geneva Convention or not. Taking advantage of the lull, the train steamed on and escaped. The Russian account is not inconsistent with this. If it be correct, not only was the Japanese force fully justified in firing, but Japan might prefer a counter-charge against the Russians of an unlawful use of the Red Cross to cover the escape of soldiers and high officials. In all probability there was no planned attempt to deceive. In the hurry of the moment all who could leave left by the only means available—a composite train. But the Geneva Convention is quite clear upon the point that the immunities accorded to the Red Cross badge are conditional upon its exclusive use to cover persons and things connected with the care of the sick and wounded. The Japanese troops would have been well within their rights if they had captured the train and all that it contained.

CHAPTER III

DAYS OF GRACE. BLOCKADING UNDER MODERN CONDITIONS

THERE are certain rights still held to belong to belligerents, which are, nevertheless, so harsh, and so out of accord with the more humane spirit of modern times, that they are invariably toned down in practice by concessions granted as a matter of grace and favour by the Governments concerned. What would happen if they were not granted passes the wit of man to discover. The rights they modify exist, like the royal prerogative of refusing assent to bills passed by both Houses of Parliament, only on condition of not being used. Perhaps some of them might be revived without much outcry. Others, especially those which restrain commerce, could not be put in force without grave danger to the power which attempted to restore them.

Among the most prominent of these rights is that of dealing harshly with subjects of the enemy found within the territory of the state at the outbreak of hostilities. Grotius, the father of modern International Law, who wrote early in the seventeenth century, says that they may be made prisoners and detained till the end of the war. In modern days the right of wholesale arrest is held to have vanished, and its place is taken by a right of expulsion. But this latter right is seldom exercised, though now and then it appears in all its former rigour, as when, at the commencement of the Boer War in 1899, the Transvaal Government expelled various categories of British subjects from the territory of the Republic. But, as a rule, enemy citizens are allowed to remain, if they live peacefully and give no aid and comfort to their own side. Sometimes they are given a certain time to wind up their affairs and leave the country. The days of grace thus accorded may be long or short, but they are always granted, unless provided for by treaty-stipulations, as a matter of favour and not of right.

The first Article of the Russian "Rules" issued on February 28, soon after the commencement of the present war, laid down that "Japanese subjects are authorised to continue, under the protection of Russian law, to reside and to follow peaceful callings in the Russian Empire, except in the territories forming part of the Imperial Lieutenancy in the Far East." The treatment thus meted out to the subjects of Russia's enemy was a compound of the new liberality and the old severity. They were free to remain in all parts of the Empire save the provinces ruled over by Admiral Alexeieff. From these they were to be expelled at once. No time to wind up their affairs, no days of grace, were given them. They were obliged to leave their homes and avocations immediately, and make for their country as best they could, in the midst of the turmoil and bitterness caused by Japan's sudden attack. What this meant in the way of robbery and cruelty we have already described (see pp.

38-40). Though things righted themselves after a time, the prompt expulsion, and the hardships inflicted on the first refugees, do not redound to the credit of the Czar's Government, or its troops and subordinate officials. No such scenes were enacted in Japan. The enemy's officials, when they left the country, were surrounded with every circumstance of courtesy and honour; while, with regard to those Russians who remained, the policy of protection on condition of registration, which was enunciated by Imperial Ordinance during the war with China, was again followed on the present occasion.

The most important commercially of the cases in which days of grace are granted occurs when, at the commencement of hostilities, belligerents gave permission for private vessels of the enemy to leave their ports unmolested within a certain time. Sometimes a right to enter as well as leave is granted. Sometimes the set period is long, sometimes short. Everything depends upon the liberality or otherwise of the combatant powers. Strictly speaking, the outbreak of war gives a state a right to capture all vessels of the enemy it finds afloat, as long as the seizure does not take place in neutral waters. Indeed, until about a century ago the custom obtained of levying, in anticipation of hostilities, what was called an embargo on vessels of a prospective enemy. That is to say, his merchantmen lying in the ports of the state which contemplated a rupture were detained, in order that there might be a rich harvest of prizes as soon as the expected war broke out. But since then the interests of commerce have prevailed over the desire for spoil. Important maritime powers, on becoming belligerents, have issued proclamations giving merchant vessels of the enemy found in their ports at the commencement of hostilities a certain fixed time during which they are free to depart unmolested. At the beginning of the Crimean War no less than six weeks were granted; and Russia allowed her days of grace to date, in her White Sea ports, from the breaking up of the ice, instead of from the issue of her Proclamation. The most liberal indulgences ever granted in this respect to an enemy's trade are to be found in the Proclamation of President

M'Kinley, issued on April 26, 1898, at the commencement of the late war between the United States and Spain. Spanish merchant vessels in American ports were allowed till May 21 for loading cargoes and departing, and were not to be captured on their return voyage unless their cargoes included contraband of war, or Spanish military or naval officers, or despatches to or from the Spanish Government. Further, enemy merchantmen who had sailed before April 21, the day on which the war broke out, from any foreign port to any port of the United States, were allowed to enter such port, discharge cargo and depart without molestation, and if met at sea on the return voyage to any port not under blockade were to be exempt from capture by American cruisers. Moreover, these liberal rules received extension from the judiciary. In the case of the *Buena Ventura* it was held by the Supreme Court of the United States that Spanish vessels came within the "intention" of the President's Proclamation if they had sailed from any American port on or before May 21, even though the departure took place before the war began. Acting on this interpretation, the Court released an enemy vessel which had sailed from Ship Island, Mississippi, on April 19, two days before the commencement of hostilities, and was captured at sea on April 22, a day after the outbreak of the war.

We look in vain for such liberality in the present conflict. The Japanese Imperial Decree of February 9, 1904, exempts from capture Russian merchantmen who leave Japanese ports up to February 16, and also those who sail direct for Japan up to that date from non-Japanese ports, and, after discharging cargo, keep on the return voyage to a route marked out for them. In every case the indulgence is made conditional upon the absence from the cargo of contraband of war. The second Article of the Czar's *Rules,* issued on February 28, granted permission to Japanese ships of commerce found in Russian ports "at the time of the Declaration of War," which was made on February 10, to remain without molestation, "for such period as may be necessary in proportion to their loading requirements, but which shall in no case exceed forty-eight hours, counting from the moment that the present declaration is published by the local authorities." The Russian indulgence, like the Japanese, was made to depend upon the absence of contraband of war from the cargoes.

We see that the days of grace granted by Japan amounted to seven only. Russia gave a variable time, it being certain that the local authorities in all parts of her vast empire would not publish the Czar's declaration on the same day. But the period of forty-eight hours, which was the utmost that could elapse between its publication and the departure of the enemy vessel, is very short, and contrasts strongly with the thirty days which might have been enjoyed under the Proclamation of President M'Kinley. It may be assumed that Japanese vessels departing in accordance with the Czar's Order are to be free from capture on the return voyage, though this is not expressly stated. But even so, their privileges are small compared with those accorded to Spanish vessels by the United States in 1898; and the case of those who were on their way to Russian ports when the war broke out is not mentioned at all. It is too early yet to pass judgment upon the whole matter. The full facts are not before us; and we do not know whether Prize Courts have pronounced on many such cases. But we can hardly escape the conclusion that commercial interests will not prove so potent to mitigate the strict rights of belligerents in this war as in other recent struggles. The sea-borne trade of Russia in the Northern Pacific is not large in extent or enormous in value. She can afford to see it suffer with equanimity. Japan, on the other hand, has much to lose. Of late the increase of her mercantile marine has been as remarkable as the growth of her fighting navy. She has taken over a large number of its best vessels to act as transports. It is impossible to exaggerate the value of such service to a state which must attack its foe with armies sent across the seas. Perhaps it was the consciousness of this which caused Russia to cut down her days of grace to a minimum. The incident should be a warning to us of what we may expect if we should be engaged in war with a maritime power. In this matter, when belligerents are bound by no definite rules of universal acceptance, they will naturally consult their own interests, though we may hope that cases will sometimes occur in which other considerations will be present to their minds. A power which sees a chance of striking a severe blow at its enemy's trade by cutting the days of grace down to a minimum, is almost certain to do so, especially if its own sea-borne commerce is so small that little is to be feared from retaliatory measures. But, quite apart from purely mercantile considerations, we must reckon here, as in many other questions, with the changed conditions of modern warfare. If a sea-going fleet is to be effective for long together, it must be followed by a train of colliers, supply-ships, repairing-vessels, and hosts of others, carrying all the numerous requirements of a navy which is a mass of complicated machinery, and is afflicted with an insatiable hunger for coal. If, on a sudden outbreak of war, a belligerent finds his ports full of merchantmen belonging to enemy owners, and well adapted for the purposes I have described, he may capture them all, dispensing with days of grace entirely, and taking full advantage of the opportunity which fortune has placed in his hands. In such a case it would be curious to see whether the desire to injure the enemy would prevail over the fear of offending neutrals, by causing a great dislocation of trade in which some of them are sure to be interested. Certainly it will be wise for British shipowners to read the signs of the times, and not calculate upon a continuance in future of the indulgences which have been accorded in recent years on the outbreak of hostilities to the merchantmen of the belligerent states. There is one class of vessel against which the full rights of war will almost certainly be exercised. I refer to swift liners, built on designs which make them easily adaptable for warlike purposes, and liable to be taken over by their governments in the event of hostilities. It would be criminal folly for a state to permit the departure of any such ships of enemy nationality which happened to be in its ports at the outbreak of a great war.

Another instance of the grant of days of grace is to be found in connection with the establishment of a blockade. When this is done effectively the result is that all neutral ships attempting to run in or out of the blockaded port are legally subject to capture and condemnation as prizes by the blockading belligerent. But it has become a general practice to allow a fixed time from the commencement of the blockade for neutral ships already in the harbour to leave it unmolested, and sometimes for those outside to enter. This has always been done in recent wars, when a blockade has been instituted soon after the commencement of hostilities, or in such circumstances that neutral shipmasters can have little or no warning. Whether it would be expected in an unusual case, like the blockade of Port Arthur and the Liau-tung peninsula proclaimed by Admiral Togo on May 26, may be considered doubtful. Ever since the beginning of February the Japanese fleet has ridden triumphant in these waters, and made attack after attack on the great Russian naval base. There can hardly be a neutral seaman in the world who did not know for weeks before the proclamation of blockade that a voyage to Port Arthur would be a most risky experiment. But putting aside anomalous cases, days of grace are expected by neutrals. Generally the indulgence is confined to ships coming out in ballast, or with cargo laden before the commencement of the blockade. But, at the outbreak of the Spanish-American War in 1898, the United States not only allowed thirty days for neutral vessels to issue from the blockaded ports, but permitted them to bring out cargo with no restrictions as to the time when it was placed on board. When Great Britain, in alliance with Germany, instituted a blockade of Venezuelan ports in December 1902, she allowed fifteen days for the departure of neutral vessels lying in the ports declared to be blockaded, and further granted to vessels which had sailed for any of these ports before the date of her notification, a period of grace varying from ten to forty days according to the character of the vessels, as sailing ships or steamers, and the distance of the starting-place from the blockaded port.

Till the end of May 1904 Port Arthur had not been blockaded in the present war. A legal blockade involves the continual presence off the blockaded port of a force sufficient to make ingress and egress very dangerous. Unless it is effective, neutral governments are not bound to submit to the seizure of their merchantmen attempting to run in or out. But under modern conditions of navigation and warfare the endeavour to make it effective is far more dangerous to the blockaders than to the blockaded, whenever there is in the port a force of torpedo-boats and destroyers able to get out, and handled with even moderate skill and dash. They ought to keep the enemy's battleships at least 50 miles away during the night, and it is at night that the attempts to run in or out will be made. The blockading cruisers may perhaps venture to patrol at 30 miles' distance, and the destroyers and torpedo-boats will be nearer still. The mosquito fleet of the blockaded side will constantly skirmish with them, and use every effort to draw them away from the channels through which it has reason to believe blockade-runners are advancing. The chances are strongly in favour of any swift vessel in an attempt to run in or out. Whereas if the commander of the blockading fleet draws his cordon of ships sufficiently near the port to make ingress or egress really dangerous, he risks their destruction by mines and torpedoes, to say nothing of the danger of their coming during a chase under the guns of any land defences. For these and other reasons the Japanese did not seek to close Port Arthur to trade by a strict blockade. The treatment accorded by the Russian authorities to ordinary merchantmen seems to have saved their foes the trouble of keeping such ships away. Vessels carrying coal and provisions were encouraged to visit the place for obvious reasons; but since it is a port of naval equipment, and shelters a fleet, the wares in question are contraband of war, and, as such, liable to capture by the Japanese without reference to any question of blockade. But I doubt whether Admiral Togo ever troubled himself much about neutral merchantmen till his proclamation of blockade was issued. He had two alternative objects. He wished either to close the channel of entrance to the inner harbour when the Russian squadron was inside, or to entice his enemy's fleet out and fight a general engagement with it away from the shelter of the shore batteries. For neither of these purposes was a blockade necessary, and accordingly the port was not blockaded. What may happen now it is impossible to say. In all probability the Japanese look upon the blockade as a temporary measure, destined to last till Port Arthur falls, and meanwhile to assist in cutting off all supplies from the garrison. If the great naval fortress is not speedily taken, blockading operations may be prolonged, in which case startling developments may take place, unless the Russian Pacific fleet is so crippled that it can be safely treated as the Americans treated the Spanish squadron in Santiago in 1898. They then stationed a comparatively small force only six miles from the entrance in the daytime, and at night brought up one of their battleships within two miles, the others being about a mile farther back in support. This was a real blockade, and a very effective one. But Santiago was not a naval port, and Admiral Cervera had no torpedo-boats and very little coal. It was possible, therefore, to take liberties with him which would not have been safe under other circumstances. Rear-Admiral H. J. May, whose untimely death in April 1904 was a loss to the Navy which only those who were privileged to work with him can fully realise, held that even when there was a great preponderance of force on the part of the blockaders, a blockaded squadron, well found and well handled, would escape five times out of six. On the sixth occasion it would be brought to battle, but with the chances of victory largely in its favour, because it would be concentrated while its opponents were scattered. These views seem borne out by both English and French experience in recent naval manœuvres. In 1901 part of the French fleet was blockaded by the rest in Ajaccio. One morning at dawn it fell upon the blockaders while they were cruising in extended formation, and was adjudged by the umpires to have defeated them. In 1902 we tried a blockade of the Greek port of Argostoli, which we were allowed to use for the purpose. The operations began on September 29, and in the night of October 4 the battleships of the blockaded squadron escaped towards the west, the cruisers having drawn some of the blockading vessels in a south-easterly direction on the false idea that they were the battleships seeking to break out. Bearing these and other instances in mind, I doubt whether we shall hear much of blockades in the present war, unless indeed the most sanguine of the Russian expectations are fulfilled, and their Baltic fleet destroys the Japanese navy. In that case it may vary the labour of protecting the transports of the victorious army which is to dictate peace in Tokio, with the diversion of carrying on a commercial blockade of the Japanese ports so as to cut off from them all external supplies. A fresh set of conditions would then come into play; and we should have a crucial experiment to clear up the problem whether, given a trade sufficiently important to make it worth while to fit out swift blockade-runners, such vessels could be intercepted by a blockading squadron of the size and power likely to be spared for the purpose by any ordinary belligerent.

CHAPTER IV

THE RESCUE BY NEUTRALS IN CHEMULPO HARBOUR. THE PROTEST OF THE THREE CAPTAINS

It is strange that the second day of the Russo-Japanese War should have witnessed the raising of a question which baffled the Hague Conference of 1899. Towards the close of the discussions on the application to maritime warfare of the principles of the Geneva Convention, Captain Mahan, who was one of the Plenipotentiaries of the United States, noticed that no due provision was made for the final disposal of those who were rescued by neutral vessels. A general right of relief and assistance was given by Articles III. and IV. to duly authorised hospital ships belonging to neutral individuals or societies. Article VI. went further and declared that "Neutral merchantmen, yachts, or vessels, having, or taking on board, sick, wounded, or shipwrecked of the belligerents, cannot be captured for so doing." Obviously the sick and wounded require attention. The first thing to do is to give them medical attention and good nursing. But the shipwrecked (*naufragés*), who are well defined by Captain Mahan as "men overboard for any cause during or after naval battles," may be strong and vigorous. And unfortunately they are likely to be numerous; as owing to the constant use of torpedoes, submarines, and mines in modern naval warfare, ships will often be sent to the bottom by a sudden shock. The immense range and deadly effect of the weapons now in use will tend to keep all who are not combatants away from the scene of action. But, on the other hand, ships fight under steam; and it may well happen that the closing shots of a battle are fired far away from the spot where the conflict began. In that case neutral rescuers may be able to attempt their humane task without obstructing the operations of the belligerents, or running into serious danger themselves. What is to be done by them with the able-bodied men they may take out of the water. The proposed Convention did not say; neither did it give any directions for the treatment of the sick and wounded after they had recovered under neutral care. It declared that those who fell into the hands of their enemies were prisoners of war; and it contemplated as a possibility the landing of the shipwrecked, wounded, or sick at neutral ports with the consent of the local authorities. In such a case Article X. provided that they must be guarded by the neutral state "so that they cannot again take part in the military operations," unless a contrary arrangement was made with the state to which they belonged. The expense of their internment, as the honourable detention described above is called, was to be borne by their own country. These directions applied to only one set of circumstances out of several which may arise; for neutral states are in no way bound to receive rescued combatants, whether sick or well, and it is obvious that some might flatly refuse to undertake the burden and responsibility of harbouring them. But, vague and incomplete as the suggested regulations were, they gave rise to so much disagreement and so many reservations on the part of important powers, that the Article which contained them was left out by general consent when the Convention was ratified. Therefore, as that instrument stands now, it binds the signatory powers to less than it did when Captain Mahan noticed its deficiencies. These he endeavoured to remedy by proposing three additional Articles, which, however, dealt only with the case of men saved from drowning by private neutral vessels. They provided that such a rescue should be deemed no violation of neutrality, but the rescuers should be bound to give up the rescued to the first belligerent ship of war which demanded them, whether the surrender delivered them into captivity or placed them again in the fighting line. If no demand were made by either side, the men were to be "considered *hors de combat*, not to serve for the rest of the war, unless duly exchanged."

These propositions failed to find favour with the Committee to which they were referred, and were finally withdrawn, lest their further discussion should endanger results already achieved. But the Plenipotentiaries expressed a unanimous wish that Switzerland would soon call a Conference with a view to a revision of the Geneva Convention. The present war in the Far East has prevented the realisation of this wish; but it is to be hoped that the return of peace will find the Powers well disposed towards the project. When such a Conference meets, the events which occurred in the harbour of Chemulpo on February 9, 1904, will form an important precedent for its guidance. Just before mid-day, the Russian cruiser *Variag*, followed by the gunboat *Koreetz*, steamed out and fought with a Japanese squadron for about an hour. They then returned in a crippled condition, and crowded with wounded men. What happened immediately afterwards it is impossible to say with absolute certainty. There were present in the harbour the British cruiser *Talbot*, the American *Vicksburg*, the French

Pascal, and the Italian *Elba*. All these appear to have given help, though to what extent is still doubtful, at least to those who have only the published documents to rely on. The American captain reports that he "sent three boats, and assisted in taking off the Russian sailors, putting them on board British and Italian vessels." The commanders of the other vessels received large numbers of Russian officers and men on board their ships; but the different accounts do not agree as to the exact circumstances in which this was done. M. Pavloff, the Russian Minister at Seoul, says: "The captain of the *Variag* sent his crew and his wounded on board the British, French, and Italian cruisers." This implies a deliberate act, planned beforehand, and carefully carried out; whereas the report of Captain Nicol to the French Minister of Marine declares that the Russians "jumped into the water, and were rescued by the European ships." On the other hand, there is no mention of such a panic-stricken rush from the injured vessels in a graphic description of the scene by "an eye-witness," which appeared in the *Daily Telegraph* of February 26, 1904. The writer evidently had exceptional opportunities of seeing all that went on. He tells us that directly the Russian ships regained the harbour, the wounded "were lowered into boats and taken to the *Pascal*, *Talbot*, and *Elba*," and then, after a time, the unhurt members of the crew were similarly ferried into safety. Even this, according to him, did not exhaust the good offices of the neutral commanders, for when at 4 P.M. the *Koreetz* exploded, "the *Variag* remained apparently unmoved, but the Russians boarded her again in the *Pascal's* boats, and set her on fire."

There can, I think, be little doubt that more was done in the way of aid than the mere rescue of drowning men; but how much more we cannot venture at present to define. It may be that the Russians would have been able without assistance not only to put their crews ashore, but to land them where they would not have fallen into the hands of the Japanese troops who had occupied the port during the afternoon of the day before. It may be that they would have been able to scuttle their vessels had they been left entirely to their own resources. The Japanese made no diplomatic protest, and therefore we may assume either that they thought it best not to raise any question as to the conduct of the naval representatives of important neutral states, or that they did not consider themselves to have been wrongfully deprived of prizes and prisoners through the action of the British, French, and Italian captains. They did, however, demand the surrender of the escaped Russians as prisoners of war. The neutral commanders demurred, and, after some time spent in negotiations, the matter was settled by an arrangement which contented all parties. The rescued seamen were taken away by neutral ships, and handed over to Russian vessels outside the area of hostilities, the Japanese Government being content for them to return to Russia on an honourable understanding that they should not be employed again during the war. Incidentally the occurrence had the good effect of removing some of the bitter feeling against Great Britain that had sprung up in Russia at the commencement of the war. The kind treatment received by the Russian sailors on board the *Talbot* evoked touching expressions of gratitude from the men themselves, their friends and relations, and their national authorities. The exchange of personal and international courtesies at such a time was a valuable contribution towards the maintenance of peace between the two countries.

The Chemulpo incident shows, among other things, that provision will have to be made in future for assistance by neutral ships of war, as well as by neutral hospital ships and ordinary neutral vessels. The nature of such provision is still open to controversy. We may hope to see the rejection of Captain Mahan's idea that neutral rescuers should be bound to give up their unhurt refugees to the first belligerent warship which demands them. Another project is that the neutral vessel which has gathered them up should report itself immediately to the belligerent commander controlling the scene of operations and take its orders from him, which would mean in most cases the surrender of the refugees as prisoners of war. This latter plan might sometimes be found difficult in practice. There have been cases when neither party controlled the scene after the action was over. The indecisive conflict between Sir Robert Calder and Villeneuve on July 22, 1805, is a case in point. Another instance may be taken from the battle of the Yalu, fought on September 17, 1894, at the close of which both the Japanese and the Chinese fleets left the waters in which they had contended. But quite apart from the fact that sometimes there may be no commander in control on the spot where the battle was fought, the principle underlying the proposals we have described seems inadmissible. It involves the deneutralisation of humanity. If the rescued men are surrendered to their own side, they will again become combatants; if they are surrendered to the other side, they will be made prisoners of war. To assist in bringing about either of these consummations is surely inconsistent with neutrality. There remain the alternatives of "internment"—that is to say, keeping them in honourable detention under neutral guardianship for the rest of the war—

or handing them over to their own friends in exchange for a solemn promise that they shall not serve again while hostilities continue. Either course seems right in principle, but if we follow the analogy of land warfare, we shall regard the former as preferable. Article LVII. of the Hague Convention Code declares that "A neutral State which receives in its territory troops belonging to the belligerent armies shall intern them." This was done on a large scale by Switzerland early in February 1871, when a beaten and starving French army, numbering no less than 85,000 men, was driven across the frontier in the vicinity of Geneva by the troops of Manteuffel and Werder. It is true that the Geneva Convention of 1864 does not contemplate the withdrawal to neutral territory of the sick and wounded combatants who are cared for in neutral hospitals and ambulances. On the contrary, it assumes that they will remain in the power of the victors. But it provides by Article VI. that those who are incapacitated shall, when their wounds are healed, be sent back to their own country, and it permits the sending back of the others also on condition that they do not again bear arms during the continuance of the war. By the "Additional Articles" negotiated in 1868 this permission was turned into an obligation; but as these articles have not been ratified, they do not bind the signatory powers. They remain, however, on record; and fortunately we have travelled in sentiment as well as in time far beyond the case of the *Deerhound*, an English yacht which rescued the captain and some of the crew of the *Alabama* from drowning, when the famous Confederate cruiser sank beneath the fire of the *Kearsarge*, off Cherbourg, on June 19, 1864. On this occasion the rescued men were landed at Southampton and there set free, so that they might, if they had chosen, have taken further part in the war; while the United States complained diplomatically that it was "direct hostility for a stranger to intervene and rescue men who had been cast into the ocean in battle." Thus both sides, with perverted ingenuity, contrived to put themselves in the wrong. We interpret the obligations of neutrality and humanity more strictly than our fathers, but we need an international agreement to give symmetry and stability to our views. When it comes to be negotiated the precedent of Chemulpo will undoubtedly make for a very wide right of rescue on the part of neutral vessels, both public and private. But we may hope it will not be pressed in favour of anything approaching a right of interference in the struggle. It is one thing to save the life of a man struggling in the water, quite another to help him in keeping himself and his ship out of the hands of the victor.

We now come to another incident connected with the series of events we have just discussed. We have already seen that on February 8 a Japanese squadron steamed into the harbour of Chemulpo and commenced to disembark Japanese troops. Early the next morning Admiral Uriu, its commander, requested the captain of the Russian cruiser *Variag* to leave the harbour, and informed him that if he did not he would be attacked. On this becoming known, the captains of the *Talbot*, the *Pascal*, and the *Elba* met in consultation. Why the captain of the United States warship *Vicksburg* did not attend the conference we do not know. He acted independently throughout. Possibly he thought, and not altogether without reason, that his colleagues were taking upon themselves responsibilities they would have done well to avoid. As a result of their deliberations, the following communication was signed by all and sent to Admiral Uriu:—

"We consider that, in accordance with the recognised rules of International Law, the port of Chemulpo being a neutral port, no country has the right to attack the vessels of another power lying in that port, and that the power which contravenes those laws is solely responsible for any loss of life or damage to property in such a port. We accordingly protest energetically against such a violation of neutrality, and we shall be happy to learn your decision on the subject."

In spite of these efforts to prevent a conflict, the *Variag* and her consort the *Koreetz* were attacked as they endeavoured to escape. What followed we have already narrated, when dealing with the rescue of the bulk of their crews by neutral boats. It remains for us now to discuss the protest and the grounds on which it was based.

Two questions arise with regard to it—Was it good in law? Was there any need to make it? The first of these involves an examination of the position of Korea as a member of the family of nations, and this we must defer to our last chapter. The second can be answered at once without reference to the conclusion we reach after discussing the first.

Assuming for the moment that what the Japanese Admiral had in contemplation was an unlawful act, we may nevertheless doubt whether it was any part of the business of the neutral naval commanders on the spot to protest against it. The question whether one neutral, or one group of neutrals, should interfere on behalf of the neutrality of another, is a matter of high policy which should be left to the Governments concerned to settle. Speaking generally, there is little reason why they should concern themselves actively in any difficulties of the kind we are considering, unless their own interests or the wider interests of humanity at large are involved.

Each state ought to use its best efforts to maintain its own sovereign authority. No grosser violation thereof can be conceived than the use of its ports and waters as a battle-ground by belligerents. If it does not exhaust all means, both diplomatic and military, in prevention and punishment, it can hardly expect other powers to trouble themselves with its grievances. Just as a man careless of his own honour can look for little zeal in maintaining it from his neighbours, so a state which makes no effort to enforce respect for its neutrality, must submit to have it disregarded without a crusade on its behalf being undertaken by other neutrals. The Korean authorities were passive spectators of Admiral Uriu's proceedings. Apparently they did not raise a finger to prevent anything that was done. In these circumstances the proper course for neutral governments was to hold themselves severely aloof. And this, as far as we know, is exactly what they have done; for the protest of the three captains does not appear to have been followed by any diplomatic remonstrances. It is, of course, easy to imagine a case in which it would be their duty to strengthen the hands of the aggrieved neutral by every means in their power, and even to insist strongly upon the preservation by it of an impartial and correct attitude. The position of China in the present war supplies an apposite instance. Any departure by her from strict neutrality would undoubtedly bring about a vast extension of the area of hostilities, and might involve several other states in the conflict. Moreover, there are in addition awful possibilities of a general massacre of Europeans, followed by the slaughterings, ravishings, and plunderings of another punitive expedition. To ward off such calamities, powerful neutral governments are justified in resorting to the strongest measures as regards China and both the belligerents. But we can all see that the case is exceptional. The rule must be one of non-interference.

As a matter of sound policy, questions which arise between neutrals and belligerents are generally left untouched by governments unconcerned in the controversy; and a latitude which they do not take can hardly be claimed by their naval officers. Among the most important of the duties these gallant servants of the state perform abroad is the protection of citizens of their own country from violence and plunder in barbarous or semi-barbarous parts of the world, and even in civilised countries during periods of revolution and mob-violence, when ordinary law and authority are in abeyance. Few people are aware of the magnificent services rendered by the British navy, as the police force of humanity, in out-of-the-way corners of the globe. The naval officer is frequently combatant and peacemaker, diplomatist, judge, and avenger all in one; and he performs these heterogeneous duties with a splendid efficiency and tactful courage which are as far beyond praise as they are too often remote from recognition and reward. If he finds himself suddenly confronted with an outbreak of what seem to him unlawful hostilities, in the course of which the lives and property of British subjects are in imminent danger, it is his duty to afford them protection by every means in his power. And if among those means he includes a timely protest against the carrying on of warlike operations in a neutral harbour, he would be well within his rights in making it. But in the case before us there was no danger threatening British, French, and Italian subjects or their possessions. The Japanese preserved perfect order, and strictly respected all the rights of non-combatants. There was, therefore, no ground for the protest, but that of high state policy; and this should have been left to the central governments to occupy or refrain from occupying at their discretion. The matter is not likely to make a precedent; and it can safely be left to sink into oblivion.

When we come to discuss (see pp. 279-285) the further question, whether there was any violation of neutrality, we shall see reason for believing that the hard facts of the case and the diplomatic verbiage whereby it was sought to smooth them over, were hopelessly at variance. Korea enjoyed a state-paper neutrality. But she was in reality the prize of war; and it was absurd to suppose that military operations would not be carried on within her borders. If this be so, there is no sound legal foundation for the protest of the three Captains.

CHAPTER V

NEWSPAPER CORRESPONDENTS AND WIRELESS TELEGRAPHY. MARINE MINES

DURING the present war the resources of science have been applied to the collection and transmission of information in a manner hitherto unprecedented, and the honour of the innovation belongs to the *Times*. It has fitted up the steamer *Haimun* with De Forest's wireless telegraphy apparatus, and placed on board a representative of its own, whose messages are sent in cipher to Wei-hai-Wei, and telegraphed from thence to London over a neutral cable. There seems no Machiavellian subtlety here, especially as the steamer is liable to search by the armed vessels of either belligerent, and has in fact been visited several times by Japanese warships, and once by the Russian cruiser *Bayan*. A searching party from the latter made a very thorough examination of the vessel on April 7. They directed special attention to the wireless apparatus, which they carefully examined. A message just sent off was shown to them; and they seem to have satisfied themselves that nothing was being done to assist the Japanese or injure the Russian cause; for they left the *Haimun* with the customary courtesies, and took no steps to detain her. But something connected with the proceedings must have got on the nerves of Admiral Alexeieff; for on April 15, 1904, the British Government received a Russian Circular to the powers, and what purports to be its exact wording was soon after cabled from Washington to the *Times*. It runs thus:—

"I am instructed by my Government, in order that there may be no misunderstanding, to inform your Excellency that the Lieutenant of His Imperial Majesty in the Far East has just made the following declaration:—In case neutral vessels, having on board correspondents who may communicate news to the enemy by means of improved apparatus not yet provided for by existing conventions, should be arrested off Kwangtung, or within the zone of operations of the Russian fleet, such correspondents shall be regarded as spies, and the vessels provided with such apparatus shall be seized as lawful prizes."

On April 20, Earl Percy, the Under-Secretary of State for Foreign Affairs, in answer to a question in the House of Commons, gave an account of Admiral Alexeieff's order, which differed by a very important word, from the American version. He spoke of "correspondents who *are* communicating information to the enemy"; whereas the phrase in the Washington telegram ran "correspondents who *may* communicate news to the enemy." There is all the difference in the world between being in a position to do an act, and actually doing it. If I am left alone in my neighbour's dining-room, I may steal his spoons; but it would be rather hard if that fact alone secured my condemnation on a charge of larceny. But let us suppose for a moment that information is actually communicated to the enemy. Then, without reference to espionage, Russia has ample means of punishing any neutral, whether newspaper correspondent or not, who sends to the Japanese from the theatre of hostilities news of the dispositions of the Russian fleet. The law of unneutral service applies to him. He is in the same position as if he had carried a despatch for the enemy, or signalled between two of his squadrons. His ship and apparatus are justly confiscate, together with all cargo that belongs to him or to the owner of the vessel. These severities might surely be deemed sufficient, even if there had been an actual transmission of intelligence direct to the Japanese commanders. But Admiral Alexeieff threatens to inflict a much greater punishment. He claims to treat correspondents using wireless telegraphy as spies, and it seems to be generally understood that he refers to those who send information by this means to their principals, and through them to the public, and not merely to any one among them who may be guilty of wafting information through the air to the enemies of Russia.

When we remember that the punishment of a spy is death, and probably death by hanging, we realise how serious is the threat of the Czar's Viceroy in the Far East. The fortune of war has left him little chance of carrying his purpose into effect; but nevertheless it is due to his exalted position, and the greatness of his country, to examine his statement carefully in the light of law and reason. Fortunately we can appeal to an authority which Russia is bound to respect.

Article XXIX. of the Hague Convention on the Laws and Customs of War on Land declares that "An individual can only be considered as a spy if, acting clandestinely, or on false pretences, he obtains, or seeks to obtain, information in the zone of operations of a belligerent with the intention of communicating it to the hostile party." Now a newspaper correspondent goes about his business openly, does not pretend to be other than he is, and, though he seeks information, his object is to communicate it to all the world, and not to the hostile party only. The particular correspondent against whom the Russian threat is aimed is the representative of the *Times* on board the *Haimun*, and in his case there is even less secrecy than usual, for it is much more difficult to disguise or hide a steamer than a man. He declares that his messages are sent in cipher to Wei-hai-Wei by a system which the instruments of neither belligerent can record, and are conveyed from thence to the office of his newspaper over a telegraphic system which neither can control. One fails to see how Japan can obtain valuable information from a cipher she cannot read, sent by means she cannot detect. Both belligerents in the present war have signed the Hague Convention, and therefore both are bound by its rules. These make a man a spy if he obtains information by secret means, and obtains it for the enemy. The methods used in forwarding it when obtained are not once mentioned, and cannot be material to the issue. And yet it is on these, and these only, that Admiral Alexeieff's denunciation turns. It may, perhaps, be argued that the Hague rules refer to warfare on land, whereas the Russian order refers to warfare at sea. But there cannot be one definition of a spy for military purposes, and quite another for naval purposes. In the matter of espionage, the accepted principles are of universal application, and it is impossible to bring the correspondent of the *Times* within them. The imagination quails before the spectacle of such a prince of journalism dangling from a yard-arm. As well might we attempt to picture the Ambassador of Russia beheaded on Tower Hill. Of course, if the unthinkable were to take place, and a representative of the *Times*, or any other paper, so far forgot himself as to penetrate secretly within the lines of one belligerent and give the information so obtained to the other, his position as correspondent would not protect him from punishment as a spy, any more than the position of an officer protects the individual who, in his devotion to his own side, penetrates the enemy's camp in disguise and sketches its defences. Article XIII. of the Hague Convention, before referred to, does, indeed, place in the category of prisoners of war, correspondents belonging to one army who are captured and detained by the other. But it refers to correspondents who are simply doing their duty as such, not to those who may be guilty of espionage; and in the case before us there was nothing of the kind. The threat of Russia bears a striking resemblance to the contention of Prince Bismarck in 1870 that Frenchmen who attempted to carry despatches in balloons from beleaguered cities were spies. Four years afterwards the Brussels Conference on the Laws of War decided that they were not, and the representatives of Germany acquiesced in the decision. The 29th Article of the Hague Code repeats it, and it is not likely to be challenged in any quarter. A similar ending to the Russian attempt to penalise wireless telegraphy may be confidently expected.

But, though the mere use of an apparatus which dispenses with wires and messengers does not constitute espionage, a case may be made out for some restraint upon the new departure in journalism which the *Times* has initiated. Yet it cannot be based upon the ground alleged by Admiral Alexeieff. The use of improved means of communication does but accelerate the transmission of news. If there be harm in this, why not penalise the electric telegraph, or even the mail train and the mail boat? In fact, the Russian reason is as weak as the Russian threat is outrageous. But the roving pressman navigating the ocean at will in a private vessel under his own direction, is free from the control exercised over correspondents attached to a belligerent army or a belligerent fleet. Before they are allowed to join they have to accept conditions laid down by the state whose forces they accompany; and they must always submit their despatches before sending them off to an officer detailed for the purpose, who exercises the widest editorial powers, including that of entire suppression. Presumably, therefore, sufficient precautions are taken to prevent any harm arising to the national cause through premature or indiscreet revelations. But there can be no such security where the collectors and senders of information are subject to no control beyond that of an occasional search of their vessels on the high seas. It is not every newspaper that is conducted with the discretion that characterises the *Times*. Every Admiral who has been in command in time of war knows how troublesome, and even dangerous, it would be for a fleet to be followed by a cloud of private ships, ever hovering round it to see what it was doing, and able to waft whatever they saw or imagined all over the world with little or no supervision. The recent action of the Japanese authorities in requesting the *Times* correspondent not to go north of a line drawn from Chifu to Chemulpo shows that they are alive to these perils. When a new Hague Conference draws up a code of rules for maritime warfare, it will have to devise regulations for such cases. We have already seen that the law, as it stands at present, provides for a right of search, and enables each belligerent to punish severely any attempt to convey information to his enemy. But more than this is needed. Power should be given by international convention to exclude the vessels of correspondents for a time from any zone of sea in which important warlike operations were in process of development. Each belligerent should have a right to place an officer on board a newspaper steamer to act as censor of its messages; and the penalty for persistent obstruction and refusal to obey signals should be capture and confiscation.

A discussion on a moot point of neutral procedure when navigating the high seas, leads naturally to a further discussion of certain matters connected with belligerent procedure in the open waters which are part of the common highway of all nations. The question, or rather the group of questions, to which we refer, grew out of the sinking of the Japanese battleship *Hatsuse*, by a marine mine on May 15, when she was cruising ten miles south-east of Port Arthur, and therefore out on the high seas a considerable distance beyond Russian territorial waters. A month before, on April 13, a Russian battleship, the *Petropavlovsk*, had been destroyed by a Japanese mine or mines. But as the catastrophe took place in the outer roadstead of Port Arthur, and at no very great distance from the shore, it was felt to be a legal, though terrible, incident of warfare. No one disputes the right of belligerents to lay mines in their own territorial waters, or those of their foes, as a means of strengthening the defences of harbours, or assisting attacks upon them. But when the area of destruction is extended to the high seas, questions of legality immediately arise. The sinking of the *Hatsuse* was discussed at once by the press of the civilised world. The general impression seems to have been that the Russians created a mine-field in the open sea, or deliberately turned mechanical mines adrift in all the waters to which they had access. Under the impression that these views were correct, Russian methods were vehemently denounced, and Russian officers charged with a gross violation of International Law. In the United States the chorus of condemnation was especially loud; but the American Government wisely refrained from making representations before it was sure of the facts, and instructed its naval *attachés* abroad to inquire into the matter.

Pending the results of inquiries and diplomatic representations of a formal or informal character, it may be useful to discuss the probabilities of the case. The ordinary observation mine which is fired from the shore by an electric current, when the enemy is seen to have come within the area of its operation, could not be anchored without great difficulty, if at all, in water as deep as that in which the *Hatsuse* sank. Moreover, the adjustment of such mines, and their connection with the observation-station on land, would require more time for uninterrupted work than is likely to be given to Russian marine engineers by the Japanese vessels engaged in watching Port Arthur. Electro-contact mines explode of their own accord when struck; but they have to be connected with a battery on shore, and the explosion takes place because the impact of the vessel which strikes them completes the electric circuit. They, too, could not be laid in deep water at any time without much trouble and great expense; and in the middle of last May, off the Kwangtung peninsula, the element of danger from the enemy would obtrude itself in a marked manner. We are, therefore, almost forced to the conclusion that the agent of destruction employed against the *Hatsuse* was a mechanical mine, which would explode, when struck, through some internal action, and would not be connected with the shore. It is just possible that the fatal blow may have been struck by a torpedo travelling at low speed and discharged at a great distance, or a submarine may have been used. There are vague reports of the existence of one or two vessels of this kind at Port Arthur; but no trace of them has ever been discovered by the Japanese, and it is exceedingly improbable that any such craft are among the defences of the Russian stronghold. Moreover, the crew of any submarine which had won for its country the greatest success that had been obtained since the commencement of the war would long ago have been honoured and decorated; and the same may be said of those who discharged the torpedo, if it was by that means that the Japanese battleship was sent to the bottom. The more the matter is considered, the more we seem thrown back upon mechanical mines as the agents of destruction. The question, then, arises, How did they come to be on the spot? Were they moored to the bottom, or were they adrift?

The former alternative is possible, but not probable. The difficulties in the way of anchoring mechanical mines in deep water are almost insuperable, and the charts show that the sea is of considerable depth ten miles from Port Arthur in the region where the *Hatsuse* sank. We cannot pretend to any certainty in the matter till further information is at our disposal; and even when official reports reach us, they may not agree. To this day there is no general consensus of opinion as to the cause of the explosion which sent the United States battleship, the *Maine*, to the bottom of the harbour of Havana early in 1898; and there exist two contradictory reports from two commissions of experts. But such evidence as we possess tends to discredit the theory of a prepared mine-field, with its lines of buoyant mines, all carefully placed at the proper intervals, and secured so as to float at the proper depth below the surface.

All other views being unlikely, we seem driven by a process of elimination to the idea that a mechanical mine left adrift was the agent of destruction in the case before us. There is ample evidence that many such mines were floating in the Korean Bay and the Gulf of Liau-tung about the time when the catastrophe occurred. On May 21 the correspondent of the *Times* on board the *Haimun* saw two within six miles of the British port of Wei-hai-Wei. Reports are current that the garrison of Port Arthur determined in their desperation to use up their stock of these terrible machines in a last reckless endeavour to damage the enemy, regardless of the risks and hazards caused thereby to neutral shipping. They therefore, so the story runs, employed Chinese junks to drop them at night in waters likely to be crossed by the squadrons of Japan. This may be a true tale, but it sounds like one of those marvellous pieces of information which are supplied to us from time to time by the gossip of Shanghai or Tientsin. Mechanical mines are very expensive, and it is not likely that the Russian naval commander in Port Arthur had enough of them in hand to enable him to sow them broadcast over the high seas. We must remember that many had been used in the earlier stages of the struggle, and many more lost. On February 11 the steamer *Yenesei* was blown up in Dalny Bay.

She was a Russian store-ship employed in laying mines. She had placed 389, and was herself destroyed by the 390th. According to a correspondent of the *New York Herald* at Chifu, the 389 were soon after blown out to sea by a great storm. If this be correct, or even partially correct, a good many of the floating mines which infest the neighbouring waters are accounted for. Then we must remember that ever since the war began both belligerents have been mining all round the coast of the peninsula on which Port Arthur stands. As the Japanese pressed their attacks more closely home, they constantly endeavoured to remove the Russian mines, and lost two or three ships in the process. We know from a telegram sent by Admiral Alexeieff to the Czar that "up to May 28 numerous Japanese mines were discovered and exploded in the roadstead." Both parties, therefore, have been hard at work removing each other's infernal machines, and it would be strange indeed if some of them did not get adrift in the course of the dredging operations. We can therefore account for stories brought back to port by frightened merchantmen, without resorting to the supposition that Russia has deliberately strewn the high seas with hidden dangers. We must not, however, forget Admiral Togo's report, that when off Port Arthur on the morning of February 9, 1904, his course was altered in order to escape a mechanical mine some 8000 yards from land, or ignore his belief that mines were laid on the spot where the *Hatsuse* sank. The Japanese even name the Russian vessel which they accuse of doing the work.

We pass now from conjecture about fact to discussion about law. Immediately we find ourselves face to face with a difficulty which is serious in all legal systems, and specially serious in that which is called International Law. There are no precedents. Mines are not new. They have been used on land since the introduction of gunpowder. But the first to employ them successfully at sea were the Confederates, who mined their harbours, and blew up several of the attacking or blockading ships. This was in the American Civil War of 1861-1865;

and since that time vast improvements have been introduced in the apparatus of submarine defence. But though mining as an art has been revolutionised, the practice of it has been confined to the ports and territorial waters of belligerent powers. The recent case is the first in which a mine acted far out at sea. How is an unprecedented situation to be met in International Law? The first thing to be done is to see whether any universally admitted principles apply to it, and, if they do, to apply them. The next is to endeavour to bring about some measure of international agreement as to future treatment of similar situations. The best method for securing this is a Conference. One is due to codify the laws of warfare at sea, as the laws of warfare on land were codified at the Hague in 1899. But we must wait for it at least till the close of the present war, and probably a good deal longer. Meanwhile discussion tends to clarify opinion; and it is certain that no new chapter will be added to the law of nations till the general opinion of the civilised world has pronounced strongly in favour of it.

International Law regards as fundamental the distinction between the high seas and territorial waters. The former are the common highway of all nations. The only purpose for which they may not be used is piracy. Even the slave-trade cannot be put down upon them without an agreement between the states concerned. Belligerents are free to carry on their warlike operations in all parts of them; but neutrals are equally free to carry on their lawful trade. Neither can set apart a zone of ocean into which the other may not intrude; yet neither can so use the right of passage as to interfere with the legitimate purposes of the other, among which purposes the operations of war must be reckoned. Wanton obstruction of one by the other is forbidden. There must be give and take on both sides.

On the other hand, territorial waters belong to the state which owns the adjacent land, and are under its jurisdiction. It throws them open to the visits of ships of all powers with which it is at peace. But it is not bound to do so, the only absolute rights they can claim in the matter being a right of asylum when in danger of destruction from the violence of wind and wave, and a right of innocent passage when the water-way between two portions of the high seas passes through the territorial zone. Neutral waters are as free from warlike operations as neutral land. The belligerents may attack each other's ports, harbours, and bays, but with this their right to perform acts of war in territorial waters begins and ends. Their power of destruction is, however, more absolute there than on the high seas; because it is not conditioned by equal rights of navigation on the part of neutrals, and moreover it has a proprietary aspect which is permanent as to their own waters, and temporary as to those which they hold in warlike occupation. They may perform in such marginal seas acts of hostility which would not be tolerated in the open ocean. No objection has ever been taken against the use of weapons which command them from the land, however destructive they may be; and when marine mines were invented they were placed as a matter of course in the ports and harbours of states which expected attack from the sea. No explicit rule of International Law gave permission; but neither, on the other hand, could any prohibition be quoted. The accepted principles were extended by analogy to the new situation. Similarly, the attacking party used without question all the means which science placed at its disposal. Nothing came of the British protest in 1861 against the action of the Federal forces in blocking up some of the approaches to Charleston and Savannah by means of vessels sunk in the channels. Mr. Seward, the American Secretary of State, replied that the obstructions would be removed when the war was over and the Confederacy vanquished, and there the matter ended. In the present war no one, even in Russia, has hinted that the Japanese went beyond their rights in attempting to block the channel leading to the inner harbour of Port Arthur by sunken merchantmen, or in mining the sea-pathway which they had observed the Russian ironclads to take when going in and coming out.

If it be right to extend admitted principles

to new cases when they are concerned with territorial waters, it cannot be wrong to use them in like fashion when we are dealing with the open ocean. Here the rule is one of concurrent rights on the part of belligerents and neutrals; and there are no ideas of proprietorship to be reckoned with, for it is held that the high seas are incapable of appropriation. Surely this rule contains an implicit prohibition of the use of such means of destruction as shall prove a lasting danger to neutral vessels, when no measures of active hostility are going on in the neighbourhood to act as a warning against approach. It has been construed from time immemorial to mean that neutral onlookers at a naval engagement are present at their own risk. It would be deemed to justify the capture, and even the destruction, of a neutral vessel which persistently hampered warlike operations. The Hague agreement for extending the principles of the Geneva Convention to maritime warfare expressly stated that belligerents might control and order off hospital ships. They might "even detain them, if important circumstances require it." If, then, warring fleets may order off, and in extreme circumstances destroy, neutral vessels which theoretically have as much right to be on the open ocean as they themselves have, conversely neutrals must be protected against the use of means of destruction which would do away with security of navigation, when issue of battle was not openly joined to be a sign to all and sundry that they approached the spot at their peril. The right to fight at sea, if it is to be conditioned, as heretofore, by the right to trade at sea, must be limited to fighting by open and avoidable means.

We will now endeavour to apply these considerations to the questions which have arisen out of the destruction of the *Hatsuse.* If she was blown up by a torpedo, discharged at close quarters from a submarine, or at long range from the shore or a torpedo boat, there was no more violation of International Law than if her magazine had been exploded by a shell from one of the forts. The torpedo was aimed directly at her, and no neutral merchantman would have been in any danger, unless she had come much closer than such vessels ought to approach to fighting ships. If the agent of destruction was a floating mechanical mine, which had got adrift owing to one or other of the operations we have already described, it is difficult to say that any existing rule of law was broken, though one may ardently desire some strong restraint upon the carelessness which strews the sea with floating death. But if a mine-field was deliberately created out in the open ocean by the Russians, in such a position that it was as likely to destroy a peaceful neutral as an enemy's warship, words fail to express the reprobation with which the act must be regarded. It is not only illegal, but cruel in the highest degree. Neutral states would be justified in calling Russia to account very sharply, and stating their intention of claiming exemplary reparation should any vessels of theirs be lost in the mined areas. The argument that, if the Japanese fleet may bombard Port Arthur from a distance of eight miles, which is far outside territorial waters, the garrison of the fortress may reply by any form of counter-attack, misses the point completely. The forts have full liberty to return shot for shot. Torpedo-attacks may be made by any means which involve attempts upon the enemy's ships and no others. But the setting of a concealed death-trap in a place where it is as likely to injure neutrals as foes is a mode of warfare contrary to all former practice and to all sound principle. The evidence available at present hardly bears out the common idea that this was done, and without the clearest proof we should hesitate to believe that such an outrage was perpetrated. The still more horrible story of the employment of Chinese junks to dump cargoes of infernal machines down upon the open sea, careless of where they floated and whom they destroyed, supposes a defiant recklessness and a wicked disregard of human life which would be a disgrace to the most hardened criminal. It is incredible without attestation infinitely stronger than vague reports.

Professor Holland has pointed out, in his admirable letters to the *Times* on this subject, that it is not always easy to know where the line should be drawn between territorial waters and the high seas. There is general agreement with regard to the marine league; but this applies to the ordinary coast-line, and not to bays, estuaries, and indentations, to say nothing of narrow straits. Some of these are dealt with by special compact. In the absence of a definite agreement, what is called the ten-mile rule is often adopted. Under it, all within an imaginary line drawn from point to point across an inlet is territorial water, as long as the line in question is not more than ten miles in length; and all outside is part of the high seas, except that the marine league is measured from the imaginary line. We cannot, however, attribute universality to this rule. The whole subject needs reconsideration. There has sprung up of late years a strong body of opinion in favour of a large extension of territorial waters. The marine league was adopted when the utmost range of cannon was three miles. It is now about twelve; and in addition artillery fire is much more accurate and destructive than it was a century and a half ago. In 1894 the *Institut de Droit International* adopted at Paris resolutions in favour of the extension of the territorial zone to six miles, with power to a neutral state to claim further extensions for the purposes of protecting its neutrality, as long as they did not exceed the utmost range of cannon mounted on its shores. In the case of bays and inlets the ten-mile line was to be replaced by one of twelve miles. The events we have been describing will give an impetus to the movement for change. Nothing can be done without an International Congress, and at present the prospect of one seems remote. Even if it were assembled, the innate conservatism of some states would be overcome with difficulty. As late as June 2, 1904, Earl Percy, the Under-Secretary of State for Foreign Affairs, stated in the House of Commons that His Majesty's Government were not prepared to recognise any extension of the three-mile limit. The arguments in favour of enlarging territorial waters are very strong; but it will be necessary to proceed with caution, lest unexpected and unwelcome results follow upon changes which were meant to promote the general good. A better example could hardly be found than was recently given by Vice-Admiral Sir R. H. Harris, when he pointed out that if belligerents were allowed to lay mines up to a ten-mile limit from their shores, and England and France were unfortunately at war, life would not be worth living for the crews of neutral merchantmen who might attempt to navigate the Straits of Dover.

CHAPTER VI

THE RUSSIANS IN THE RED SEA. THE USE OF NEUTRAL WATERS BY BELLIGERENTS

THOUGH the Russo-Japanese war has lasted but a short time, it has shown that many difficulties may arise in connection with the visits of belligerent squadrons and single ships to neutral waters. Some of these troubles are old friends with faces not indeed quite new, but much changed owing to the influence of steam and improved weapons. But behind them there stand others in thick battalions—not troubles that have happened, but troubles that may happen, nay, that are sure to happen in future. Naval warfare has been revolutionised in the last forty years. The use of neutral ports as rendezvous for torpedo-craft with a view to a sudden dash at an enemy many miles away will raise grave questions, as will also submarine warfare, and the conveyance of information by wireless telegraphy from vessels lying in neutral harbours to vessels far out at sea. These are but examples of what may happen, and do not pretend to be an exhaustive list. They are mentioned in order to show that our administrative authorities, aided by enlightened public opinion, ought to consider these matters while we are at peace, and elaborate a policy for the country to carry out in a great war, whether we are belligerents or neutrals. But the object we have before us now is the less ambitious one of studying cases that have arisen lately. From this point of view we shall find very useful a short account of the doings of the fleet under the command of Admiral Wirenius during the first few weeks of the present war.

When hostilities began, the Czar's squadron from the Mediterranean was on its way to reinforce the naval strength of Russia in the Far East. Most of the vessels were at anchor by the island of Jebel-Zukkur, in the south of the Red

Sea, and the remainder lay at Jibuti, the capital of French Somaliland. In three or four days all assembled at Jibuti, where they remained for about a week. At the end of that time official news of the commencement of hostilities reached the local authorities, and the Russian Admiral was told that he must leave. This he did in thirty-six hours, having coaled meanwhile from his colliers in French waters. By this time he had received orders from his Government to return, along with all ships of the Russian Volunteer Fleet which were on their way to the scene of action. Accordingly, he proceeded up the Red Sea, stopping and searching merchant vessels on his way. Three neutral ships laden with coal were detained as prizes, two of them being British, the *Frankby* and the *Ettrickdale*, and one Norwegian, the *Mathilda*. All carried steam coal of the kind used by men-of-war. Two were undoubtedly destined for Japan, one directly, the other after touching at a neutral port. With regard to the final destination of the third there might be some doubt, though the circumstances were suspicious. These prizes were brought into the Gulf of Suez, within Egyptian territorial waters. There they were kept about four days, and meanwhile their captors used the anchorage as a base from which to overhaul neutral ships navigating the Gulf. The Egyptian Government protested against this use of its waters. Meanwhile, the Czar telegraphed an order for the release of the colliers, because they had been captured before coal was declared contraband by Russia. This conciliatory action, and the departure of Admiral Wirenius for the Mediterranean and the Baltic, simplified matters considerably; but no sooner had the ships passed through the Canal than a fresh complication arose. They asked for coal at Port Said, on the plea that they required it in order to reach Cadiz on their journey back to Russia. Their request having been granted, one of them, the *Dmitri Donskoi,* used the coal for cruising purposes. For some days she hung about the approaches to the Canal, where she overhauled several vessels (see *Consular Report,* Annual Series, No. 3229, July 1904). This was a gross breach of faith, especially as her commander had signed a declaration whereby he undertook upon his honour that his ship would proceed "at once and by the direct route" to Cadiz. It is satisfactory to refer here to Mr. Balfour's statement on July 29, 1904, that coal would in future be refused to any belligerent vessel which behaved in a similar fashion. The refusal should apply further to any ship commanded by the officer who broke his word.

It is quite clear that Admiral Wirenius exceeded his rights, and violated the neutrality of Egypt in a gross and open manner. No proximate acts of war may take place in neutral waters, and they may not be used as a base of operations. Further, neutrals may make all reasonable rules to protect their sovereignty over their own territorial waters, and may refuse the prizes of the contending parties admission to their ports. This Egypt did in her Neutrality Order of February 10, and she also forbade the use of her waters "as a station or place of resort for any warlike purpose." It was the duty of the Russian Admiral to respect the rules of International Law, and also the regulations laid down by the neutral government, seeing that these latter were reasonable in themselves and applied impartially to both sides. Instead of this he anchored his prizes in Egyptian waters about twenty miles below the port of Suez, and, keeping his fleet in the same situation, sent out vessels to waylay passing merchantmen. It is to be hoped that the timely protest that was lodged against these proceedings will prevent a recurrence of them during the war. Incidentally they raise another question, which is partly a matter of law and partly a matter of policy. It may be argued that the narrow opening of the Gulf of Suez, and the smallness of the navigable channel throughout its whole extent, makes it territorial water. But seeing that it is twelve miles wide at the entrance, and has generally been accounted a part of the high seas, too much stress should not be laid upon the contention that it is already an Egyptian bay. But, if it is not, should it not be made one by International agreement, in order to protect the neutrality of the Suez Canal, or, better still, be made to share the permanent neutrality of the latter? By the Convention of 1888 the entrances to the Canal are not to be blockaded, and no acts of hostility are to be committed in the channel or in the sea to a distance of three marine miles from either end of it. These rules might be observed to the letter, while a squadron stationed in the Gulf of Suez, where the navigable channel does not exceed eight miles in width, practically kept the entire passage from sea to sea under belligerent control. This is a much more important matter than it appears at first sight. Nothing less than the neutralisation of the Canal is involved. The Russian squadron which used the Gulf of Suez as a cruising-ground in February, 1904, was able in its narrow waters to intercept merchantmen reported to them by their Consul at Suez as fit to be stopped. They were not interfered with in the Canal or within three miles of its southern terminus, but nevertheless the passage was almost as completely blocked as it would have been by a belligerent force in possession of the town and harbour of Suez. The Gulf of Suez is but a natural prolongation of an artificial waterway. It is useless to neutralise the latter without neutralising the former also. Once out in the wider expanse of the Red Sea, a trading vessel could take her chance of search and seizure under the ordinary rules of maritime warfare. But to lure her into a narrow cut on the guarantee of a solemn international pact that it is perfectly free even in time of war, and then leave her to be captured in another passage which opens out from the first and is itself too narrow to give a prospect of escape, is a sure way to deprive sea-borne commerce of the benefit ostensibly conferred upon it by the Convention of 1888. It is true that no extreme inconvenience was caused in February. Yet we must remember that the Russian squadron was in difficulties about coal, and hardly knew what to do with its prizes. Moreover, it was on its way home, and therefore its stay was short. But Russia in this war, or in a future war some other belligerent, may place in the Gulf an efficient force, strong enough to seize merchantmen, and capable of sending its prizes without difficulty into a port of its own country for adjudication before a prize court. In that case every rule of International Law would be strictly obeyed. The Convention of 1888 would be observed with absolute exactness. And yet the neutralisation of the Suez Canal would have vanished like a dream. The situation deserves the careful consideration of the maritime powers. It is ripe for a fresh agreement.

Severe criticisms have been published in England on the conduct of the French authorities in permitting the Russian fleet to remain for so long a period in Jibuti, and allowing the ships to fill their bunkers with coal before they departed. Most of them are based upon the assumption that International Law forbids belligerent vessels to enjoy the shelter of neutral ports for more than twenty-four hours at a time, and, further, that it limits supplies of coal to the quantity which will enable the recipients to reach the nearest port of their own country. This is an error, but one so general that those who give expression to it have much excuse. All the more reason, therefore, is there for an attempt to set forth the correct view. International Law draws a clear distinction between what neutral states must do in these matters and what they may do. Among the things they must do is to forbid fighting in their ports and waters, or the use of such ports and waters as a base of operations. They must not allow belligerents to ship supplies of arms and ammunition therein, or recruit men, or increase their warlike force. Speaking generally, we may say that a belligerent ship must not leave a neutral port a more efficient fighting machine than she entered it, except in so far as increased efficiency may come from increased seaworthiness or a better supply of provisions. On the other hand, neutrals may permit the supply of things necessary for subsistence, and they may repair in these ports and waters damage due to the action of the sea. A distinction is drawn between what is necessary for life and what is necessary for war. It is not very logical, because a man must live before he can fight, and those things which keep him in health fit him to perform his duties as a combatant. But, such as it is, it has to be observed. Moreover, it follows from the fact that belligerents have no absolute right to the hospitality of neutral ports, that neutral governments may make conditions of entry, and impose a time-limit upon the stay of combatant vessels in their waters, and a limit of quantity upon the supplies of things necessary for subsistence and navigation, such as coals and provisions, which they are still permitted to furnish or not at their own will. Whatever regulations they may make as to these matters are binding upon belligerents as long as they are not unreasonable, and are enforced impartially on both sides.

If we apply these principles to the case before us, we shall see that France was not bound by International Law to turn out Admiral Wirenius and his ships after they had enjoyed the hospitality of the port of Jibuti for twenty-four hours. Quite apart from the alleged absence of official information of the outbreak of war, there was no obligation upon her to do anything of the kind. But what she did for Russia she is bound to do for Japan. If in future a Japanese squadron desires to stay for some time in a French port, to compel their departure at the end of a day would be a breach of neutrality, unless, indeed, they were using it as a lurking-place from whence to sally forth to the attack of Russian vessels. Similar considerations apply to coal. The French Circular of Neutrality, issued on February 18, 1904, limited permissible supplies and repairs to those necessary for "the subsistence of the crews and the safety of the navigation," and forbade the use of French waters for warlike purposes, or for the acquisition of information, or as bases of operation against the enemy. It may be doubted whether anything done at Jibuti was outside a reasonable construction of these words. A full supply of coal was allowed, but there was no returning again and again for shelter and further supplies. It would be hard to say that the port was used as a naval base. Unless and until a Japanese fleet is refused the facilities granted to the Russian squadron, there is little ground to reproach France with a violation of neutrality.

But it will be said Great Britain is stricter. We do not allow, by our Rules issued from the Foreign Office on February 10, 1904, a longer stay than twenty-four hours to belligerent vessels visiting our ports and waters, unless they have obtained permission to take innocent supplies or effect repairs, in which case we turn them out as soon as they are ready to depart. Nor do we permit them to take more coal than is necessary to carry them to the nearest port of their own country, "or to some nearer named neutral destination," and no two supplies of coal for the same vessel are to be allowed in British ports at lesser intervals than three months. All this is perfectly true. Great Britain, and the important group of states who have followed her example in this respect, have chosen the more excellent way. Their definite rules are very much to be preferred to the vague phrases of the French Circular. But while the law of nations allows the stay of belligerent vessels in neutral ports, and sets no limit upon the amount of coal that may be supplied therein for purposes of navigation, we have no right to accuse a friend and neighbour of unneutral conduct because she does not copy our wholesome restrictions. States are bound by International Law, not by British regulations, however excellent they may be.

The case of coal is peculiar and unsatisfactory. There is great need of a further advance in the rules which deal with it. Before the application of steam to navigation no one gave it a thought in connection with warlike purposes. Belligerent ships were as little likely to ask for it as they are to-day to demand granite or sand. But when, in the middle of the last century, the navies of the world changed from sailing vessels to steamships, it suddenly became immensely important. Yet the law of nations, based upon the practice of nations, still regarded it as an innocent article which might be supplied to any belligerent ship whose commander was so curiously constituted as to want it. But in 1862 Great Britain led the way in an attempt to put it on a more satisfactory footing. Taking advantage of the power possessed by neutrals to make reasonable regulations for their own protection, she issued in the midst of the great American Civil War a number of rules which dealt, among other matters, with supplies of coal. They were limited almost exactly as they are in the present war. We have kept to our rules ever since, when neutral in a maritime struggle; and several powers, notably the United States, have adopted them. Meanwhile, coal has become much more important for warlike purposes than it was in 1862. Without it a ship-of-war is a useless log. It is as essential for fighting as ammunition, and much more essential for chasing or escaping. Moreover, the great increase in the size or speed, or both, of modern vessels causes them to consume it in much greater quantities than before. A belligerent which can obtain full supplies of it in neutral harbours gains thereby an enormous advantage. The neutral may be perfectly willing to grant similar supplies to the other side, but its wants may never be so great, and consequently the assistance given to it may never be so effective. Besides, it is of the essence of neutrality that no aid should be given to the belligerents, and this is by no means the same thing as giving aid to both equally.

The present war will possibly supply us with an object-lesson to illustrate this great truth in a most vivid and convincing manner. Russia is now fitting out her Baltic fleet with the intention of despatching it to the scene of conflict. But the long voyage from Kronstadt to any port in her Asiatic dominions which may remain in her possession at the time chosen cannot be accomplished without frequent supplies of coal. How are they to be obtained? The Czar has no possessions of his own along the line of route. But his ships might coal first at some English port, then in a Spanish harbour, then in turn at Port Said, which is Egyptian; Jibuti, which is French; Achin, which is Dutch; and Canton, which is Chinese. Colliers could meet the fleet at various points, and some states would probably allow coaling from them in their waters. Others might not; but in fair weather coal can be taken on board at sea, and there is always the possibility of shelter among uninhabited islets. The accounts recently received of the proceedings of the *Ural* and the *Don* off the coasts of Spain and Portugal indicate experiments on these points. Moreover, the warships might sometimes be towed by other vessels. Taking all things into consideration, and bearing in mind that the facilities for coaling in some of the ports indicated may be small, it nevertheless seems likely that the Baltic fleet could perform the voyage to the Far East, though it would probably arrive with foul bottoms and empty bunkers. The colliers which met it would be liable to capture as enemy vessels if Russian, and as carriers of contraband if neutral; but the danger is more nominal than real, for probably Japan would not detach cruisers to intercept them in distant seas. Thus by making full use of neutral facilities, Russia can circumnavigate the greater part of two continents, and throw against her enemy a great naval force, whereas, if she had to trust entirely to her own resources, the fleet in question could not come within several thousand miles of its foe. No neutral, in the plan before us, grants the Russian vessels permission to take in supplies more than once. Unless we hold that coaling is forbidden when the coal would be used to take to the scene of hostilities a fleet which could not otherwise proceed thither, no rule of International Law is infringed, and even the stricter British regulations are not broken. Yet Japan is exposed thereby to a great danger. Doubtless neutral states would treat her as we have supposed them to treat Russia. But she is not at all likely to send a squadron into the Baltic. Clearly it is a case of *summum jus, summa injuria.* Under the forms of law the spirit of neutrality is violated.

Can anything be done in this matter to bring legal rules up to the standard of enlightened international morality? In England a strong body of naval opinion would support the prohibition of all supplies of coal to belligerent vessels in our ports. But, though this is the ideal to be aimed at, not only for ourselves but for the whole civilised world, it may be doubted whether many states are yet ripe for so great a change. We can, of course, set the example; but if it is not followed, no appreciable progress is made, while we assume a fresh burden when neutral, and reap no benefit when belligerent. We have to remember that France has not yet come up to our standard of forty years ago. Her policy with regard to coal in warfare is to place no restrictions upon the trade in it. The word is not to be found in her recent Neutrality Circular. Evidently the thing is reckoned among the supplies which a belligerent vessel may

K

receive in neutral waters, though the quantity taken at any one time would probably be limited by the rule which confines such supplies to what are necessary for the security of navigation, while the too frequent repetition of occasions of coaling would be checked by the provision against the use of any French port as a base of operations. But, taken at their best, French rules require strengthening; and the question for us to consider is whether a further advance on our part would be more likely to bring our neighbour into line with us, or confirm her in her present position. No doubt our interests would be served by complete prohibition, if it could be made general; and for this reason other states may decline to follow any lead we may give. As we are better off for coaling-stations than any other power, and have greater facilities for keeping our fleets supplied by colliers, we could not fail to benefit by a change which would make men-of-war dependent upon coal obtained in their own ports or from their own supply-ships. On the other hand, we have more to lose than most states by the present system. Our sea-borne trade is so enormous, and so essential to our welfare, that an enemy could do vast damage by means of two or three swift and well-handled commerce-destroyers, which might for a time obtain coal in neutral ports, though we had succeeded in closing all their own against them. Our neighbours are well aware of this; and they know in addition that the change, if made, would either greatly restrict their operations at sea, or lay upon them the necessity of acquiring distant coaling-stations. All things being considered, we could hardly expect many of them to follow us in adopting a rule of total prohibition, in spite of its manifest necessity from the point of view of perfect and impartial neutrality, and its desirability as tending to curtail the area of war. To make it and apply it in complete isolation would, as we have seen, operate against us in two ways. It would restrict our trade in coal when neutral—a result which would doubtless appear undesirable to the great majority of us, though the more thoughtful might welcome a rule which prevented to some extent the transfer to other powers of a resource which cannot be replaced, and ought to be carefully husbanded for our own defence. Further, it would not, when we were at war, restrain our enemies from obtaining supplies in neutral ports, because, by the supposition on which we are arguing, no country but our own would prohibit them. The conclusion seems forced upon us that we had better not try to act alone, and that at present there is little chance of persuading other powers to join us. But the matter should be kept in view by our rulers, and whenever opportunity offers to induce a group of maritime states to make the change, it should be taken without hesitation. It may come if at some future time a powerful belligerent, who has suffered severely by the grant of large coaling facilities to its enemy, pursues France, or any other of the laxer powers, with persistent claims for reparation, following the precedent of the United States against Great Britain in the matter of the *Alabama* and her sister cruisers.

But if the absolute refusal of coals to combatant vessels in neutral ports is for the moment outside the scope of practical international politics, it behoves us to inquire whether there are any alternative means of improving upon the present unsatisfactory state of affairs. The Scandinavian kingdoms of Sweden and Norway, and Denmark, have applied a drastic remedy. By a Declaration of Neutrality published early in May, but dated February 13 of the present year, they have closed their ports to the public vessels of both belligerents, with the exception of hospital ships. Further, they have notified all whom it may concern that submarine mines have been laid down along their coasts, in view of a possible extension of hostilities to the adjacent seas. No doubt a state does possess a right to exclude belligerent vessels from its harbours and roadsteads, if it can show good cause for such a denial of the usual hospitalities. In the case before us the weakness of the states concerned is sufficient reason for their action. It would be far easier to admit a Russian squadron into a Danish or Norwegian port than to control them when there, or to get them out if they were determined to stay. In all probability the concurrence of stronger neutrals, and possibly even of the belligerents themselves, was obtained before the notification was issued.

But what is possible for the small Scandinavian realms is not possible for great and powerful neutral states, which cannot abdicate their position in the world by issuing a declaration which would amount to a confession of inability to keep order in their own waters. Are they therefore left without resources for the improvement of existing rules on the subject of supplies of coal to belligerents? By no means. The Egyptian Neutrality Order of February 10, 1904, points out a way; and we shall not be going far astray if we ascribe its adoption to British influence. The Order provides that before the commander of a belligerent ship-of-war is allowed to obtain coal in any port of Egypt, he must obtain a written authorisation from the authorities of the port, specifying the amount he may take. Such authorisation is to be granted only after the receipt from the commander of a written statement, setting forth the name of the port to which he is to go next, and the amount of coal he has at the moment in his bunkers. He will then be permitted to take what is sufficient for the purpose declared to be in view, and no more. Here, then, we have the germ of a new and better rule; but it requires extension before it can be pronounced entirely satisfactory. Short as experience under it has been, the possibility of evasion has been abundantly demonstrated. The action of the *Dmitri Donskoi* (see p. 115) in using the coal obtained to carry her to Cadiz for the quite different purpose of cruising off the Mediterranean entrance to the Suez Canal, and overhauling neutral merchantmen who were voyaging to and from it, shows that some further security is required. Moreover, what the Russian cruiser did in February does not stand alone. It can be paralleled from the practice of the *Alabama*. Throughout her career she never entered a Confederate harbour, but continued to cruise against the commerce of the United States all over the world by the aid of supplies of coal obtained in British and other neutral ports. In her case, however, no written declarations were required, and consequently there were none to be ignored. The danger of misuse of coal obtained from neutrals is clear. It is granted for purposes of navigation, and it can easily be used for purposes of fighting or chasing. Even such emphatic declarations as the Egyptian authorities require can be violated by unscrupulous officers. There should be added to the rule demanding them a clause to the effect that any use of the coal obtained by means of them for cruising purposes, or for steaming to a different destination, unless in the event of chasing or being chased on the way to the appointed place shall disqualify both the vessel and her commander from receiving further supplies in any port of the same neutral during the same war. This would put an end to evasions; and though it could not prevent such a scandal as the voyage of a Russian fleet from the Baltic to the Northern Pacific by using neutral harbours one after another as coaling-stations, it would render the process more cumbersome, and make the problem of the final arrival of the squadron in fighting trim so much more difficult of solution that in all probability it would never be attempted.

It must not be supposed that the present war has seen no questions connected with the use of neutral waters except those raised by the cruise of Admiral Wirenius and his squadron. Unfortunately for herself, the *Mandjur*, a Russian gunboat, was lying in the neutral harbour of Shanghai at the outbreak of hostilities. The Japanese naval authorities promptly sent the cruiser *Akitsushima* to watch the mouth of the Yang-tse off Woosung. Stationed there, she blocked the only way whereby the *Mandjur* could reach the open sea and the Port Arthur fleet. The position was certainly a trying one for the Russian commander. China, the territorial power, exercised its undoubted right as a neutral and ordered him to leave within twenty-four hours. Full in his path lay an enemy of greatly superior force. If he departed, he went to certain capture or destruction. If he remained, he broke international law by defying a neutral government. He chose the latter alternative. The Chinese executive was too weak to risk the consequences of determined action. They might have detained the gunboat for the rest of the war, or fired upon her if she persistently declined to move, or escorted her out to sea, leaving her to take the chances of battle or escape when well outside territorial waters. But they did none of these things. Instead, they parleyed. Japan, on the other hand, might have given notice to China that she would no longer respect the territorial waters of a state which seemed powerless to defend its neutrality, or she might have claimed reparation for the indulgence shown to her opponent. But she was extremely anxious not to drive matters to extremities, and to stand well with China and the rest of the world. So she too parleyed; and as the result of a sort of three-sided negotiation between herself and China on the one hand, and Russia and China on the other, the gunboat was dismantled so thoroughly as to make her permanently useless, and the *Akitsushima* was then withdrawn from her long watch at the mouth of the Yang-tse. This happened at the end of March. Mild measures proved in the end effective. A difficult situation was terminated without bloodshed and without international complications. The Japanese Government reaped at last the reward of its mingled forbearance and firmness, in the loss of a ship to the enemy and the freeing of its own cruiser for more exciting and important enterprises.

CHAPTER VII

CONTRABAND OF WAR. THE RIGHTS OF BELLIGERENTS AND NEUTRALS WITH REGARD TO IT

THE latter part of the previous chapter seems to lead up naturally to a consideration of the great subject of contraband of war. We saw in it that munitions of war were goods of so special a character that neutral states were bound by International Law not to allow them to be taken on board belligerent ships lying in their ports. We also saw that coals were regarded in many quarters as possessed of the same character to a lesser extent. They need not be prohibited altogether, but severe restrictions are laid upon the supply of them. The question naturally follows, Are there not other articles of commerce like those that have been mentioned in their fitness for warlike purposes? And when this has been answered in the affirmative, the further inquiry suggests itself, Is the trade in all these articles as free and open as the trade in things whose primary and ordinary use is of a peaceful nature? It is not; and the attempt to explain in what way, and to how great an extent, it is restricted, lands us in the midst of the law of contraband. We can discuss the main principles thereof without much use of legal phraseology. Stripped of technicalities, they can be understood easily by all who are capable of forming an intelligent opinion on international affairs; while without some knowledge of them no one ought to presume to give an opinion at all on questions which public men are now discussing everywhere, such as those connected with our supplies of food from abroad.

We have first to bear in mind that the contraband character attaches to goods on account of their usefulness for warlike purposes. No one doubts that a case of rifles or a battery of artillery found on their way to the custody of a belligerent power are destined for its army or navy. They may be intended to shoot big game or decorate public parks, but the possibility is too remote to be worth entertaining. They are always contraband of war. On the other hand, no one doubts that a cargo of pianos or children's toys are destined for peaceful purposes. They may possibly be found useful for building a barricade or kindling a bivouac fire, but here again the possibility is too remote to be worth entertaining. They are never contraband. Other goods, however, do not bear their character on their face. One may look at a stoutly-built horse till it drops, without discovering whether it is intended to draw a dray or an artillery waggon. One may examine a telegraph wire till sight fails, without being able to tell whether it is assigned to military or civil use. It is with regard to goods of this kind, articles useful for warlike and peaceful purposes indifferently, that difficulties arise. The general trend of Continental opinion is against making these contraband in any case. But Great Britain and the United States hold that the use to which they will be put determines their character, and that this use is to be inferred from the predominant characteristic of their port of destination, as commercial or naval, and other surrounding circumstances. Articles of this kind we call conditional or occasional contraband. Articles useful primarily for warlike purposes we speak of as absolutely contraband.

But something more than the character of the goods has to be considered before it is possible to decide whether or no they are contraband of war. We have to inquire into their destination. There is a considerable trade in arms and ammunition at all times. A cargo of them found at sea is not necessarily on its way to the enemy. The same thing is true of the materials and machinery for making them, which are as noxious as the completed articles. Before goods can be treated as contraband it must be shown that they are travelling to an enemy destination. It need not be a port of the enemy's country, though ninety-nine times out of a hundred it is. An enemy's ship-of-war or fleet on the high seas will do as well. Indeed it has been decided that a hostile squadron lying in a neutral port is an enemy destination, and the decision is generally regarded as good in law. A camp, garrison, or army of the enemy also fulfils the necessary conditions. We omit, as being too technical and complicated for our present purpose, questions connected with the Doctrine of Continuous Voyages, and sum up what has gone before in the statement that, in order to make goods into contraband of war, a hostile character and a hostile destination must coexist.

We are now in a position to define the nature of the offence we are discussing. It is not what it is so often and so wrongly called, selling contraband. Anybody may do that with absolute impunity so far as International Law is concerned. It is carrying contraband. This is forbidden to neutral merchants, ship-owners, and ship-masters, on penalty of the confiscation of the contraband goods and all other portions of the cargo which belong to the owners of the contraband. The ship also may be confiscated by a Prize Court, if it and the noxious goods are subject to the same ownership, or if there has been any attempt to evade search or deceive the captors. A neutral government which shipped munitions of war in its public vessels to one of the belligerents would be guilty of a most gross breach of neutrality. But it could not be dealt with as a private individual. The goods, if captured, would undoubtedly be confiscated; and then a diplomatic question, which might possibly end in war, would arise between it and the belligerent who suffered by its misconduct. The ordinary law of contraband deals with neutral individuals, not with neutral governments.

But when a neutral individual engages in the trade of carrying contraband, the proper authority to act against him is the belligerent who is injured by his venture, not his own government. States at war are very apt to complain of a contraband trade which reaches any considerable dimensions, and frequently call upon neutral authorities to restrain their subjects from carrying munitions of war to the enemy. But such requests are not granted. Neutral governments point out that the law of nations does not hold them responsible for the ordinary trading transactions of their people, though they are bound to prevent the enlistment of men and the departure of warlike expeditions which have been fitted out within their territory or territorial waters. Belligerents must be their own policemen. Each has the right to capture neutral vessels engaged in carrying contraband of war to its enemy. It may seize them on the high seas, in its own waters, or in those of its enemy; and when the seizure has taken place, the contraband goods are always confiscated, and the ships which carry them often share their fate. The proper agency for effecting the confiscation is a Prize Court, which is a court of the captor's country, sitting in its territory, and deciding according to International Law. We need not discuss the exceptional cases when prizes are not brought before a court for adjudication. It is sufficient to say here that a neutral has a right to a legal judgment when his property is seized at sea by a belligerent, and when such judgment has been given it is conclusive as to the vessels and goods concerned. A neutral subject engages in contraband trade at his own risk. His government will not protect him, unless it deems the seizure unlawful on account of the place where it took place, or the circumstances in which it was made, or the innocence of the goods seized. This last reason is more common than any other. The natural tendency of belligerents is to regard doubtful things as contraband and treat them accordingly; while neutral states are drawn in the opposite direction, and resolve the doubt in favour of the innocence of the disputed articles. In the case of serious disagreement, the neutral government protests first against the inclusion of the goods in question in the belligerent's list of contraband. Then, if they are not withdrawn from the list, it declares that it will not recognise the legality of the condemnation of such goods when owned or carried by its subjects. Finally, if, in spite of its representations, condemnation takes place, it claims damages from the belligerent government for unlawful seizure and confiscation. Probably a settlement of some sort is arrived at sooner or later. Failing anything of the kind, retaliatory measures can be adopted. Only in the very gravest and rarest cases would war be justifiable.

We are now in a position to examine the differences between the two belligerents in their treatment of the present subject. According to the Prize Law of Japan, as set forth in Appendix VII. of Professor Takahashi's book, *International Law during the Chino-Japanese War*, contraband goods are divided into two classes. The principle of division is maintained in the notification published by the Japanese Government on February 10, 1904, though the goods placed in each class differ somewhat from the list published ten years ago, and the words which express the distinction between the two classes are also varied. The first class are contraband "when passing through or destined for the enemy's army, navy, or territory," the second only when "destined for the enemy's army or navy, or in such cases where, being goods arriving at the enemy's territory, there is reason to believe they are intended for the use of the enemy's army or navy." That is to say, a distinction is drawn between goods in their own nature so fitted for warlike purposes that it is morally certain they are meant for warlike use, and goods the use of which is uncertain, and may vary according to circumstances. The first are to be prevented from reaching the enemy at all, the second only where it is clear they are destined for the use of his armed forces. In other words, the Japanese have adopted the British doctrine of contraband, though they have not given it the wide scope to be found in our Admiralty Manual and the Prize Court decisions on which that document is based. There can be little doubt that, though our main principles are correct, we have sometimes applied them with undue severity. The Admiralty list of goods absolutely contraband is much too long, and includes articles, such as spars and anchors, which certainly ought to appear among goods conditionally contraband. Our brave and thoughtful allies have improved on their model in this matter, as in so many others. Their list of contraband goods of the first class—what we should call goods absolutely contraband—is short. It contains only "military weapons, ammunition explosives, and materials (including, lead, saltpetre, sulphur, etc.) and machinery for making them, uniforms naval and military, military accoutrements, armour-plated machinery, and materials for the construction or equipment of ships of war." A clause at the end adds: "All other goods which, though not coming under this list, are intended solely for use in war." It is true that these words are general, but no exception can be taken to their purport. Goods of the second class—our conditional contraband—are set forth with similar brevity. They are enumerated as "provisions, drinks, horses, harness, fodder, vehicles, coal, timber, coins, gold and silver bullion, and materials for the construction of telegraphs, telephones, and railways." There is nothing here that can be deemed excessive. From the point of view of neutrals, the lists are satisfactory; and our experience of the war of ten years ago gives no ground for supposing that Japan will administer her rules in an oppressive manner.

It is impossible to speak so confidently with regard to Russia. She makes no distinction between goods absolutely contraband and goods conditionally contraband. With her all goods that are contraband at all belong to the former category. Her Government stated this unreservedly on the 28th of February of the present year. Such a declaration might be in no way offensive to neutrals, if the list of contraband goods were short, and contained only articles of use primarily and ordinarily for warlike purposes. But Russia's list is not short, and it contains goods which are technically classed as articles *ancipitis usus*, that is to say, useful indifferently for warlike and peaceful purposes. In order to find out exactly what the Government of St. Petersburg considers to be contraband of war we have to study Appendix II. to Section 14 of the *Instructions approved by the Admiralty Council, September 20, 1900*, and Article VI. of the *Rules which the Imperial Government will enforce during the war with Japan*, which are dated February 28, 1904. Roughly speaking, the list of 1900, which we are told was drawn up as long ago as 1877, is reproduced, with some alterations and many important additions, in the list of 1904, which runs as follows :—

1. Small arms of every kind, and guns, mounted or in sections, as well as armour plates.

2. Ammunition for firearms, such as projectiles, shell-fuses, bullets, priming, cartridges, cartridge-cases, powder, saltpetre, sulphur.

3. Explosives and materials for causing explosions, such as torpedoes, dynamite, pyroxyline, various explosive substances, wire conductors, and everything used to explode mines and torpedoes.

4. Artillery, engineering, and camp equipment, such as gun carriages, ammunition waggons, boxes or packages of cartridges, field kitchens and forges, instrument waggons, pontoons, bridge trestles, barbed wire, harness, etc.

5. Articles of military equipment and clothing, such as bandoliers, cartridge-boxes, knapsacks, straps, cuirasses, entrenching tools, drums, pots and pans, saddles, harness, completed parts of military uniforms, tents, etc.

6. Vessels bound for an enemy's port, even if under a neutral commercial flag, if it is apparent from their construction, interior fittings, and other indications that they have been built for warlike purposes, and are proceeding to an enemy's port in order to be sold or handed over to the enemy.

7. Boilers and every kind of naval machinery, mounted or unmounted.

8. Every kind of fuel, such as coal, naphtha, alcohol, and other similar materials.

9. Articles and material for the installation of telegraphs, telephones, or for the construction of railroads.

10. Generally, everything intended for warfare by sea or land, as well as rice, provisions, and horses, beasts of burden and others which may be used for a warlike purpose, if they are transported on the account of, or are destined for, the enemy.

We must add to the above raw cotton, which was declared to be contraband by Imperial Order on April 21; and we have to remember that to every article in the list, whatever its character, is applied the rules which we apply to our "goods absolutely contraband." It will be condemned if found in a neutral ship voyaging to an enemy destination, no matter whether such destination be a commercial or a naval port; no matter whether it is destined for civilian or military use. We English discriminate. According to our practice, when many classes of goods capable in their own nature of a double use are found under a neutral flag on their way to an enemy destination, they are confiscated if the port to which they are bound is one where war-fleets are fitted out, or equipments for armies received, and released if it is devoted to peaceful commerce and the supply of the civilian population. And, further, even when we seize and confiscate, we pay the owners a fair price for the conditional contraband so taken, and also for goods absolutely contraband which are raw material and the produce of the country in whose merchant ship they are found. It is only when the goods are not raw material and not the produce of the country exporting them, and yet are absolutely contraband, that is, useful chiefly and almost exclusively for warlike purposes, that we appropriate without compensation. Yet our practice has been deemed harsh and indefensible. Continental jurists and statesmen have condemned it in no measured terms. The *Institut de Droit International* discussed the question at its meeting at Venice in 1896, and declared against our doctrine of conditional contraband, but added: "Nevertheless, the belligerent has at his option, and on condition of paying an equitable indemnity, a right of sequestration or pre-emption, as to articles which, on their way to a port of the enemy, may serve equally for use in war or in peace." This, in effect, not only concedes our view, but even goes dangerously far beyond it. We do not seize at all unless we deem the goods destined for warlike use. The wording of the resolution of the *Institut* would allow seizure and pre-emption whenever the articles *ancipitis usus* were on their way to a port of the enemy, without regard to the purposes they were likely to fulfil.

Russia has, however, contrived in her recent regulations to unite all severities and throw off all restraints. Our Doctrine of Conditional Contraband vanishes, but only in order that the class of goods it covered may be placed in the list of those absolutely contraband. The *Institut's* recommendation of sequestration or pre-emption is ignored, and all goods in the list, harmful and harmless alike, are to be subject to seizure without compensation.

It might have been argued in the spring of 1904 that the Czar's ministers would have little opportunity of putting their rules into action. No doubt appearances favoured this view; but, as the late Lord Beaconsfield once said, "War changes like the moon"; and we have lived to see our trade severely harried. Belligerents have a right to make their own lists of contraband; but neutrals have a right to object to them, or any part of them. As humble citizens of a great nation interested more than any other in the freedom of sea-borne commerce, we may venture to suggest that the diplomatic action which has already been so fruitful in some matters should be continued with regard to others. Remonstrances need not be unfriendly, even though they be earnest; and that there is need for plain speaking this chapter and the three following will show. The treatment of all goods deemed contraband as equally noxious is a blow at neutral trade which we did not venture to strike, even in the height of our conflict with Napoleon, when we certainly did many unjustifiable things. It is reasonable to suppose that the enormous trading interests of modern times are powerful enough to secure for sea-borne commerce better treatment than it received in the days of Lord Nelson and Sir William Scott.

CHAPTER VIII

ARE COALS, PROVISIONS, AND COTTON CONTRABAND OF WAR? THE DUTIES OF NEUTRAL GOVERNMENTS WITH REGARD TO THE TRADE IN SHIPS

WE are now in a position to consider certain specific questions, which could not be treated in a satisfactory manner without some preliminary knowledge of the law of contraband and the attitude of both the present belligerents with regard to it. We will take first the treatment to be accorded to neutral cargoes of coal, found by cruisers of one belligerent on their way to the ports or ships of the other. Russia's record with regard to this important matter is remarkable for inconsistency. The West African Conference of 1884-1885 decreed freedom of commerce and navigation for the Congo River, even when the riparian powers were at war, excepting, however, contraband articles from the operation of this salutary rule. In December 1884 the Russian representative at the Conference astonished his colleagues by declaring that his Imperial Master would not regard coal as one of the articles so excepted. Russia thus ranged herself with France in maintaining the extreme view that coal could under no circumstances be regarded as contraband of war. Great Britain and the United States hold that it is contraband when destined for naval or military use, but innocent when destined for commerce, manufacture, or domestic consumption. Japan has adopted this doctrine by placing coal in the second class of her contraband goods, which means that she will subject it to capture only when it is caught on the way to the war-vessels of the enemy, or a hostile port of naval or military equipment. Germany takes either this position, or the still more marked one that coal on the way to the enemy is contraband, irrespective of the nature of the port where it is to be delivered. Till recently, then, we had France and Russia in agreement in holding coal to be in no case contraband, and Great Britain, at the head of a group of important maritime powers, maintaining that it belonged to the class of conditional contraband. But on February 28, 1904, twenty days after the outbreak of the present war, Russia quietly boxed the compass, and proceeded to substitute one extreme view for the other. The Eighth Article of her *Rules which the Imperial Government will enforce during the war with Japan* included in her list of contraband "every kind of fuel, such as coal, naphtha, alchohol, and other similar materials." We have to remember that all the articles enumerated in Russia's rules are "unconditionally contraband." Bearing this in mind, we see that a cargo of soft coal proceeding from Newcastle to Yokohama for the use of the civilian population of Tokio is subject to capture and confiscation at her hands, as much as a cargo of smokeless coal proceeding from Cardiff to Nagasaki for the use of Admiral Togo's fleet. Have we any reason to object? The answer to this question requires to be thought out very carefully. What follows is offered as a contribution towards the thorough discussion which is necessary before a final decision is reached.

We saw in the last chapter that the total prohibition of supplies of coal to belligerent warships in neutral ports was a thing to be aimed at, both on account of its intrinsic justice and also because such a rule would redound to the interests of our own country, if it were engaged in a great naval struggle. But if our Government took this view, and endeavoured to induce other neutrals to join with us in forbidding such supplies, it might be met by the objection that we do not look upon coal as contraband of war always and in all places, but rank it among those articles which we deem contraband or not according to circumstances. Lord Lansdowne voiced the usual British doctrine with admirable clearness, when he wrote in February last to a Cardiff firm, "Coal is an article *ancipitis usus*, not *per se* contraband of war; but, if destined for warlike as opposed to industrial use, it may become contraband." Can we hold this position, and yet press for the placing of coal on the same footing as ammunition, so far as belligerent men-of-war visiting our territorial waters are concerned? No doubt we should be told that if such ships are no longer to be allowed to buy coal in our ports, we can hardly claim for our merchantmen the right to carry it to their ports unmolested, as long as they are not ports of naval equipment. And yet this argument does not seem conclusive. An article of commerce may be so essential for hostile purposes that no warship ought to be supplied with it in neutral waters, and yet so essential for the ordinary purposes of civil life that it ought not to be prevented from reaching the peaceful inhabitants of belligerent countries. The two propositions are not inconsistent. If both are upheld in reference to coal, we can work for the abolition of the present liberty to supply it to combatant vessels when visiting neutral ports and harbours, and at the same time maintain that when it is sent abroad in the way of ordinary trade, belligerents must treat it as conditionally and not absolutely contraband. But at present, as we have seen (see pp. 129-132), there can be no question of complete prohibition. All we can hope to gain is a rule which will deny coal in future to war-vessels when they have broken the conditions on which neutrals allowed them to take a supply. Such an advance in strictness would in no way conflict with our existing doctrine that coal is properly placed among goods conditionally contraband.

The foundations of this doctrine are remarkably strong. Undoubtedly coal is an article of the first necessity in warfare. Therefore it is absurd to contend, as Russia did till lately, that it can never be contraband. But it is equally necessary for peaceful purposes. Civilised mankind cannot do without clothing, prefers its food cooked, and needs warmth in its houses. For all these purposes fuel is essential, and over very large areas coal is the only fuel available. Therefore it is absurd to contend, as Russia does now, that coal is always contraband. We are forced to the conclusion that sometimes it is contraband and sometimes it is not, the difference turning upon the difference in the purposes for which it is destined. It is quite true that belligerent captors cannot determine these with absolute accuracy. The cargo bound for a commercial port may go on by rail to a port of naval equipment. The hard coal, so suitable for the furnaces of warships, may be really intended to supply manufacturing and domestic needs. But, after all, the rough-and-ready tests, which are the only ones possible in war, will yield correct results nine times out of ten, and the tenth must be accepted with resignation as one of the untoward incidents of a desperate game. We did well to take our stand upon the position so clearly defined by the Secretary for Foreign Affairs in February. Great Britain and the United States let Russia know, courteously but firmly, that they did not intend to submit to the condemnation of any of their coal cargoes, unless they were clearly destined for the warlike purposes of Japan; and the result was that Russia, while maintaining her own view, promised in September a lenient application of it.

We now come to the question of provisions, on which a good deal of light will be thrown by a short historical review. At the outbreak of the war between Great Britain and France in

1793, both parties first adopted, and then under neutral pressure abandoned, the practice of capturing as contraband neutral cargoes of provisions on their way to open commercial ports of the enemy. Out of this attempt, and its failure, grew the doctrine that food was not contraband unless it was destined for a besieged place or an armed force of the enemy. This view met with general acceptance until 1885, when France, hitherto one of its most conspicuous adherents, gave notice to neutrals that in the course of her then existing hostile operations against China she would confiscate, as contraband, rice conveyed in neutral vessels to any Chinese port north of Canton. Our Government immediately demurred, and restated the old view. Hostilities terminated before a case of seizure arose, and therefore the controversy never came to a decision. But two points should be noticed with regard to it. Prince Bismarck stated, in reply to a memorial of complaint from a number of Hamburg merchants, that it belonged to belligerent powers to say what they intended to regard as contraband. And, again, the action of

France was defended at the time, and has been defended since, on the ground that the rice in question was tribute paid to the Chinese Government, and used by them in lieu of money for the pay of their soldiers. This argument has the merit of ingenuity; but it is capable of such enormous extension that few commodities would be safe from confiscation under it if they could be looked upon as national property. The sale of tobacco, for instance, is in many countries a state monopoly. Would it not be easy to say that tobacco-cargoes bound for the ports of these states must be regarded as contraband, because their value would by and by find its way into the government treasury? All articles of commerce can be expressed in terms of money, and since state treasure is contraband, the goods which represent it could be regarded as contraband also. A list of contraband goods compiled on this principle might easily grow so great as to cripple neutral trade in articles of the most innocent character; but whether the argument be good or bad, the fact that it has been put forward, and the further fact that Prince Bismarck pointedly refrained from scouting the French claim, should warn us that we must look carefully to our own position, since it is a matter of the utmost importance for us to keep our imports of food free from molestation at all times.

The action of Russia in the present war emphasises the warning. Hitherto she has been on the side of the received rule. Food-stuffs were absent from her list of contraband of 1900. But the additions of February 28, 1904, contain rice and provisions. We are glad to know that our Government followed the example of their predecessors in 1885, and entered a strong protest. In the action of Japan there is nothing of which we can complain. With her food is contraband only when destined for the use of the enemy's armed force, and, I presume her courts would add, for a besieged place. When American steamers laden with canned meats and other provisions put into Japanese ports on their way to Port Arthur and Vladivostock at the beginning of the war, their cargoes were, of course, seized. There was no breach of International Law in such acts. The only comment it is possible to make upon them is that on these occasions some of our American cousins showed a strange lack of their usual sagacity in matters of commerce.

Our own policy is perfectly clear. Unless we alter our habits fundamentally, or diminish our numbers by more than half, we cannot live upon the produce of our own soil. We might, indeed, adopt the suggestion of Professor W. J. Malden, and plant four million acres with potatoes; but, like other counsels of perfection, this stands a better chance of admiration than adoption. Practically, we are dependent upon imports from abroad for about four-fifths of the wheat and flour we consume. Of this enormous quantity no very large proportion comes from our colonies and dependencies. In the eight years ending with 1903 it varied from 8 to 24 per cent. In these facts we find at once our call to action and our hope of success in action. The value of our food trade to other nations secures that we shall receive powerful assistance in our efforts to keep it open. It is a matter of life and death for us to prevent any change in International Law which shall make the food of the civilian population undoubtedly contraband, and, if arguments and protests will not do it, force must. Should the use of force be necessary, we are not likely to stand alone. Our trade in food is so lucrative to the great wheat-producing and meat-producing countries that they will strain every nerve rather than lose it. The satisfaction of our appetite for food is also the satisfaction of their desire for gain. Our kinsmen of the United States are with us heart and soul in the doctrine that food-stuffs are not contraband unless destined for warlike use, and they are prepared to enforce it at all risks. It is highly probable that if, in time of war with France or Germany, American corn-cargoes bound for Liverpool were captured on the high seas, the Stars and Stripes would soon wave side by side with the Union Jack over the fleets which swept the commerce-destroyers from the ocean. Other countries know this as well as we, and in that knowledge, and the efficiency of our navy, lie our chief securities.

There is no need to dwell for long upon the recent addition by Russia of cotton to her list of contraband goods. We are told that her declaration to that effect refers "only to raw cotton suitable for the manufacture of explosives, and not to cotton yarns or tissues." It is difficult to see how the raw cotton destined for the manufacture of explosives is to be distinguished from the raw cotton destined for the manufacture of shirtings or pocket-handkerchiefs. We in England certainly have no good ground for protesting against the capture of what is intended to be made into a most terrible instrument of warfare. In the Admiralty *Manual of Naval Prize Law* the materials for ammunition are ranked along with ammunition in the list of goods absolutely contraband. If Russia means to seize and confiscate no cotton except that which she can prove to be on its way to a Japanese military or naval workshop, there to be manufactured into a powerful explosive, neutrals have no cause of complaint against her. But in that case her recent declaration seems superfluous; for the "Rules" issued by the Imperial Government on February 28 enumerated "explosives and materials for causing explosions" among the articles then declared to be contraband.

Moreover, gun-cotton itself was mentioned in them under its scientific name of pyroxylin. Thus the completed article and the substances from which it is made were already penalised, when the recent declaration against raw cotton was published on the 6th of May. It may be that nothing more was intended than to remove every possibility of doubt by making a perfectly explicit statement. But, if that were so, the object in view was not attained, for the explanation itself required to be explained immediately. The term "raw cotton" is quite general. As it stands it includes all the lint which comes from the bolls of the cotton plant. A diplomatic gloss declares that only such of it as is suitable for the manufacture of explosives is intended. If we add that it must be destined to be so manufactured, as well as suitable for the purpose, we have reduced the declaration to proper limits. The action of Russian cruisers and Russian courts should be carefully watched, to make sure they do not step beyond its terms thus interpreted. As long as these are observed, no illegal hardship will be inflicted on neutral trade. But the moment they are overstepped a branch of innocent commerce which is specially important in the Far East is subjected to a most unwarrantable interference. The conciliatory action of Russia with regard to the cruisers of her Volunteer Fleet (see pp. 205-218) gives reason to hope that neutral susceptibilities will be considered in other matters.

The attempt to quote the action of the United States Government in the great American Civil War, in order to justify Russian action, supposing it to have been directed against cotton in general, is singularly unfortunate. In the summer of 1861 the Confederacy took full advantage of the fact that practically the whole of the world's supply of cotton was grown in the Southern States. The sale of it was put under severe restrictions so as to secure the greater part of the crop for the government. It was then used to supply the means for the purchase abroad of ships, arms, and ammunition. Agents of the authorities at Richmond shipped thousands of bales to Liverpool, where it was sold at a high price, and the proceeds drawn against to pay for warlike stores.

In these circumstances the Northern generals did not treat cotton as private property, exempt by the laws of war from seizure and destruction. Instead, they burned all they could find in their invasions of Southern territory, and there can be no doubt they were justified in regarding it as a war-supply of the enemy, and therefore subject to whatever severities they thought fit to employ. Their government went further, and declared cotton to be contraband of war. There are grave doubts of the legality of this extreme step; but we may point out that, even assuming it to have been perfectly correct, it affords no justification for proclaiming all raw cotton to be contraband now, in the present state of the war in the Far East. If the soil of Japan grew a large part of the raw materials for the cotton looms of Europe, if the Government of Japan had possessed itself of most of the crop, and if the armaments and warlike stores of Japan were purchased by the proceeds of the sale of the bales so held, then indeed the two cases would be sufficiently similar for the first to be a valuable precedent. But, as things are, there is not the slightest resemblance between them. Japan grows no cotton. She imports from the United States what she requires for her manufactures. Even if the conditions were reversed, and Russia followed the example of the United States by declaring all cotton to be contraband, strong arguments would be forthcoming to show that the declaration could not be justified by International Law. Cotton belonging to the Japanese Government, and found voyaging in Japanese ships, would, of course, be subject to capture as enemy property. But if it were found in neutral ships, could it be captured as contraband? In the first place, there would be no belligerent destination, for by the suppositions on which we are arguing, the cargoes would be on their way to some neutral manufacturing country. In the second place, cotton is harmless in itself and could only be seized as representing specie. Can it be maintained that the law of nations recognises these substitutions of one thing for another in order to turn innocent into noxious goods? We have already seen to what lengths the process may be carried (see p. 165). At one time the argument runs:—Rice equals money; money, when the property of the state, is contraband; therefore rice, when the property of the state, is contraband. At another time it is:—Cotton equals money; money, when the property of the state, is contraband; therefore cotton, when the property of the state, is contraband. And so we may go on and on, jauntily resolving into contraband one article after another that has in itself little or no connection with warlike uses, and at each step inflicting some fresh disability on neutral trade. Equations are very useful in mathematics. In International Law they look like unmitigated nuisances. It is submitted that the claim of the United States to regard cotton as contraband in 1861 was wanting in legal justification; and that any similar claim which Russia may make in the present war would be still more unlawful. In all probability no such claim has been made, or will be made. The very different statement that raw cotton "suitable for the manufacture of explosives" will be deemed contraband of war may be allowed to pass with the reservations already set forth.

Early in 1904 it was almost impossible to

open a newspaper without coming upon a paragraph to the effect that some government or some private individual had sold or was about to sell some vessel or vessels to the Russian Government, or to some one who was more than suspected of being its agent. Vagueness was the distinguishing mark of most of these paragraphs. The few that were definite were generally contradicted within a week of their first appearance. But later the reports became more precise and better authenticated. There can be little doubt that large purchases have been effected and important contracts entered into. The objects in view seem to have been the strengthening of the Baltic fleet for a voyage to the Far East, and the fitting out of a number of cruisers to attack the trade between Europe and Japan. The problems raised by this method of obtaining commerce-destroyers, transports, and store-ships are intensely interesting, and the various ways in which purchase may be effected, joined with the varying degrees of warlike efficiency in the vessels when purchased, render them very complex.

The matter cannot be discussed in a satisfactory way unless we break up the main problem into parts and consider each separately. We must begin by making a distinction between what the individual may do and what the state may do in the way of selling to foreign governments, and then we must draw a further distinction between what the state is bound as an honest neutral to prevent and what it may allow its subjects to do at their own risk. When we have settled these two points we shall be in a position to answer some of the questions raised by the attempt of one, if not both, of the present belligerents to obtain warships by purchase during the continuance of hostilities.

Among the ordinary functions of the state trading is not included, whereas it is reckoned among the ordinary functions of the private person. A neutral government which enters into a bargain with a state at war for the transfer to it of military or naval stores, or ships suitable for military or naval purposes, is deliberately going out of its way to provide its neighbour with instruments of warfare, and by so doing violates its neutrality in an open and scandalous manner. So strongly has this been felt for a long time past, that when in 1825 the Swedish Government discovered that six frigates it had sold to an English firm were about to be transferred to an agent of Mexico, which was then in revolt against Spain, it immediately cancelled the transaction and refused to deliver the vessels. And again, when in 1863 an old gunboat, the *Victor*, sold by the British Government to a private firm, reached the hands of Confederate agents, who made an unsuccessful attempt to fit her out under the name of the *Rappahannock*, orders were given that no more ships of the Royal Navy should be sold during the continuance of the American Civil War. A still more remarkable case occurred in the same year. By an arrangement between Great Britain and China a flotilla of gunboats was built in England and taken out to China, manned by British sailors, and commanded by a British officer who was to enter the Chinese service. On his arrival differences arose between him and the Chinese authorities, and he declined the appointment. Rather than leave the vessels in the hands of China at the imminent risk of their being sold to the Southern Confederacy, the British Government took them over and recouped China to the extent of more than £100,000, the difference between the original value of the gunboats and the price they fetched when sold after the close of the war. These are remarkable cases. They prove beyond a shadow of doubt that modern governments do not feel themselves at liberty to sell warships, or vessels that can be made into warships, to belligerents, whether they are full-fledged states like Russia and Japan, or insurgent communities striving to become states, like Mexico in 1825 or the Southern Confederacy in 1863. It may perhaps be too strong to say that a state is absolutely bound to stop its ordinary sales of disused stock from its dockyards and arsenals in time of war, lest belligerent agents should be among the buyers, though no doubt such intermission would be the better and safer course, but the duty of refraining from any special bargain of purchase and sale with either of the powers at war lies clear and distinct upon it. This duty, however, applies only while hostilities are going on. The sale of the two cruisers now called the *Nisshin* and the *Kasuga* to Japan by the Argentine Government was perfectly legal, because it was completed before the war began. For the same reason Italy committed no breach of neutrality in allowing the departure of the vessels from Genoa; while, as for Great Britain, the silly stories about the use of the British flag and the escort of British ships of war in the Mediterranean, were disposed of once for all by Lord Selborne's emphatic denial in the House of Lords on February 25. It is true that ex-officers of the Royal Navy were in command of these cruisers when they left Genoa, and remained in command after the outbreak of war, which took place while the ships were on their way to Japan. But the British Government has no more control over servants who have left its service than it has over ordinary citizens. On this occasion it dissociated itself from their action in a marked way, by striking their names off the emergency list of ex-officers who are available in time of war.

Neutral individuals are not subject to all the restraints which rightly fall on neutral governments. If they happen to be traders they are in no way bound to suspend or limit their commercial transactions because a war is going on. As Jefferson pointed out when complaints were made in 1793 of the activity of American merchants in supplying France with munitions of war, "Our citizens have always been free to make, vend, and export arms. It is the constant occupation and livelihood of some of them." But he went on to say that every belligerent had a right to confiscate such portions of these arms as it could capture on the way to ports of its enemy, and added significantly, "To this penalty our citizens are warned they will be abandoned." This brings us to the second point we have to investigate—the distinction between what a neutral state may permit its subjects to do at their own risk, and what it must prevent them, and indeed all residents within its territory, from doing, in order to vindicate its own neutrality. In what follows we will confine ourselves almost entirely to the case of ships, since it is with them that present difficulties have arisen.

It is no business of a neutral government to interfere with the trade in contraband of war carried on by its subjects; but, on the other hand, it may not interfere to protect them from the confiscation of their contraband goods when on the way to a belligerent destination. Speaking generally, we may say that its duty is to sit still and attend to its own affairs. But it cannot always confine itself to passive non-interference. When the acts of those under its control amount to more than mere trading, and become something akin to active participation in the war, then it must step in and prevent its territory from being made the starting-point of expeditions or the base of operations.

Now a ship is something more than a mere article of contraband trade when she is built or fitted for purposes of warfare. She has become a warlike expedition, and immediately a duty with regard to her is placed upon the neutral government. It is bound by

International Law to prevent her departure from its ports on her mission of hostility against a neighbour with which it is at peace. And surely the obligation is not limited to ships whose mission it is to fight. Transports or colliers come under it equally with men-of-war. In order more effectually to fulfil this duty states sometimes arm their governments with authority to prevent even the building in their ports of such vessels as we are discussing. Our own Foreign Enlistment Act does this; but herein it goes beyond the law of nations. As Sir William Harcourt said in his note appended to the Report of the Neutrality Commission of 1867, "To build is nothing, unless the vessel be armed (a better expression would have been, adapted for war), and despatched; it is in these acts that the real breach of neutrality consists." The first of the Three Rules of the Treaty of Washington of 1871 expressed the same view when it said that a neutral state was bound to use due diligence "to prevent the departure from its jurisdiction of any vessel intended to cruise or carry on war as above (*i.e.* against a power with which it is at peace), such vessel having been specially adapted, in whole or in part, within such jurisdiction for warlike use."

If this view be correct, our Government is bound, as long as the war lasts, to prevent the departure from this country of the two Japanese battleships for the construction of which contracts were signed with two British firms at the end of January in the present year. The Foreign Enlistment Act gives them ample power for this purpose, and there can be no doubt that it will be exercised. Other states are under the same obligations, which, as we have seen, are imposed by International Law, and therefore bind all the members of the family of nations. When therefore we read of large purchases by Russia of swift liners from the North-German Lloyd and the Hamburg-America Companies, we waited somewhat impatiently for the announcement that the vessels in question would not be permitted to depart from German jurisdiction. But it never came. Instead a considerable fleet of auxiliary cruisers, acquired in the manner described, took the seas in the late summer under the Russian flag, and proceeded to search neutral vessels for contraband in the South Atlantic. They are lightly armed, and could not cope with a hostile warship. But they are quite capable of dealing with merchantmen, and will probably continue their career unimpeded, unless and until Japan can despatch a few of its swiftest cruisers to African and European waters. It will be said that they were purchased as ships of commerce, and received their equipment for war in Russian ports. But it may be argued that their size and speed, together with their fittings for the conveyance of passengers, constituted an adaptation for warlike purposes, even if none of them were built for guns, as is undoubtedly the case with some of the German liners. Moreover it is impossible to believe that the vendors were ignorant of the purposes for which their vessels were bought. The least one can say in the matter is that a claim on the part of Japan against the German Government would find strong support in recent developments of the law of neutrality.

CHAPTER IX

ARE MAIL-STEAMERS PRIVILEGED? WATERWAYS UNDER SPECIAL REGULATIONS. NEUTRALITY AND WIRELESS TELEGRAPHY

EARLY in May of the present year the Russian armoured gunboat *Krabri* stopped and searched the British mail-steamer *Osiris* when on her voyage between Brindisi and Port Said. The object of the search was to discover the Japanese mails; but none were found, either because there were none, or because the search-party did not light upon them. After two hours the *Osiris* was allowed to proceed, and on her arrival at Port Said on May 4 she at once reported the incident. A section of the English press commented very strongly upon it, and the general opinion seemed to be that the Russian warship had greatly exceeded her rights.

Various grounds were put forward in support of this view. In some quarters it was argued that belligerents had no right to search neutral vessels so far from the scene of hostilities. The mental habit of manufacturing International Law as required, out of the feelings of the moment and an intuitive sense of the equities of the case, is responsible for this assertion. There is no such limitation upon the Right of Search. By the common law of nations it applies everywhere, except in neutral territorial waters, and to all neutral merchantmen except such as may be exempt by special favour. Whether the *Osiris* came within this class we will discuss by and by. Meanwhile, in order to disabuse men's minds of the notion that a space-limit is set upon the belligerents' right to stop and search private vessels flying a neutral flag, we will quote a notice issued to mariners by the Board of Trade in the middle of last March. It refers, as will be seen, to the high seas generally, and is perfectly explicit as to the duty of submitting to search. Its words are: "Masters of British merchant vessels must immediately stop or heave to, when summoned on the high seas to do so by a warship of either belligerent, and must not resist being visited or searched for contraband of war by such warship, as any attempt on their part to evade or resist visit or search may be attended with serious consequences to themselves and to their vessels and cargoes."

Another and much more arguable point has been taken, not against search in the Mediterranean generally, but against the particular search we are now discussing. It refers to the undoubted rule that a belligerent has no business to use the waters of a neutral as a base of operations for warlike acts; and it points out that as Russia has no ports of her own in the Mediterranean, the *Krabri* in all probability came out from some neutral port when she started to intercept the *Osiris*, and returned to that port when she had performed her task. It is also probable that the supplies of coal which enabled her to place herself in the path of the mail-boat were obtained in the same port. The case is certainly one for inquiry. It would be intolerable if a belligerent vessel was allowed to use a neutral port as a lurking-den from whence to harry the commerce of other neutrals. On the other hand, it would be foolish to affirm that, because such a vessel had obtained coal in neutral waters in order to enable her to reach her next port of destination, therefore she must not make use of any portion of that coal to chase and stop a merchantman she happened to meet while in the *bonâ fide* prosecution of her voyage. It will be wise to wait for fuller information before we make up our minds on this point.

But, even though there be no good reason for objecting to the search by belligerents of neutral merchantmen in general, the question arises whether the fact that the *Osiris* was a mail-steamer does not give her special immunities. In attempting an answer we may put aside the few anomalous cases where the mail-boats are public vessels, but carry passengers and merchandise as well as letters. The Ostend boats are examples. They are the property of the King of the Belgians as reigning sovereign. In the case of the *Parlement Belge* it was decided that the subordinate and partial use of them for trading purposes did not take away their public character and deprive them of the immunities which belonged to them by virtue of it. Whether this doctrine would be extended to cover exemption from belligerent search in time of war, it is impossible to say with certainty. But we may be sure that, if such vessels should in future be held free from molestation on the same footing as ordinary public vessels employed exclusively on state business, the neutral power whose ships they are will be made responsible for any abuse of their immunity by carrying contraband of war or performing unneutral services. They are, however, so exceptional that we may leave them out of account. Ordinary mail-steamers are simply merchantmen of a particular kind, owned by private persons, and carrying mail-bags by contract with the state, as one department of their trade.

In recent times a practice has grown up of granting special favours to such mail-boats in time of war, if they are neutral and willing to accept the conditions imposed. The United States has been the pioneer in this matter.

During her war with Mexico she allowed British mail-steamers to pass unmolested in and out of the port of Vera Cruz, which came into her possession for a time in 1847. In 1862, when the American Civil War was at its height, the Government of Washington exempted from search the public mails of any neutral power, if they were duly sealed and authenticated, but it was added that the exemption would not protect "simulated mails verified by forged certificates and counterfeit seals." If a vessel carrying mails rendered herself subject to capture for other reasons, she might be seized, but the mail-bags were to be forwarded unopened to their destination. The example thus set was followed by France in 1870. At the commencement of her great war with Germany she announced that she would take the word of the official in charge of the letters on board a regular mail-steamer of neutral nationality as to the absence of any noxious communications. The Proclamation of President M'Kinley at the beginning of the war with Spain in 1898 went further still. It declared that "the voyages of mail-steamers are not to be interfered with, except on the clearest grounds of suspicion of a violation of law in respect of contraband or blockade." A similar indulgence was granted by Great Britain in the course of the Boer War to steamers flying the German mail-flag. They were not to be stopped on mere suspicion that there might be unlawful despatches in their bags. On the other hand, many modern cases may be mentioned where no indulgence, or a very limited one, was given. For instance, in 1898 Spain did not duplicate the American concession, and in 1902 Great Britain and Germany would not allow neutral mail-steamers to pass through their blockade of Venezuelan ports, but stopped them instead, and after overhauling their correspondence and detaining what seemed noxious, sent the rest ashore in boats belonging to the blockading squadron.

We see then that practice is by no means uniform. It is impossible, therefore, to argue that the usage of the last half-century has conferred upon the vehicles of the world's commercial and social communications an immunity from belligerent search which they did not before possess. The utmost we can venture to assert is that such a usage is in process of formation, and is in itself so convenient that it ought to become permanent and obligatory, due security being taken against its abuse. This last condition will be difficult of attainment. No government agent on board a mail-steamer can be aware of the contents of the letters for which he is responsible. There would be a terrible outcry if he took means to make himself acquainted with them. His assurance, therefore, as to the innocence of the communications in his bags can be worth but little, even though it is given in all good faith. States must face the fact that to grant immunity will mean that their adversaries in war will use neutral mail-boats for the conveyance of noxious despatches made up to look like private correspondence. Probably it will be worth while to take the risk of this rather than dislocate the affairs of half a continent by capturing and delaying its correspondence. While general freedom was given, it might be wise to reserve a right of search and seizure in circumstances of acute suspicion.

At present nothing of the kind has been done. Our Government has no right to demand from Russia that our mail-boats be left unsearched by its cruisers. But it may represent that great inconvenience will arise if the right of search is enforced in its naked severity, and ask both of the powers at war to make concessions similar to those which we made at Germany's request in 1901. There is no need to go so far as the United States have recently gone in the Barrundia case and subsequent incidents of the like kind, when they claimed for their mail-steamers a privileged position with regard to political refugees who had taken shelter on board them. We do not want to assimilate the mail-packet to the warship, but we do desire to establish the principle that the innocent correspondence of neutrals all over the world shall not suffer because two powers have seen fit to break the peace. And we are more likely to succeed by means of quiet diplomatic pressure and courteous reasoning than by heroics about an outrage which was no outrage at all, but at worst a discourtesy. It may be well to add here that neither private correspondence nor diplomatic and consular correspondence is regarded as noxious matter. Only despatches relating to naval and military affairs come within that category, and subject the carriers to pains and penalties.

In stopping and searching the *Osiris* by means of one of the ships of her regular navy, Russia did no more than exercise in a harsh and reactionary manner a right which belonged to her as a belligerent power. She would have been better advised had she granted some of the concessions to neutral mail-steamers which have been so frequent of late years. The United States made no sacrifice of dignity when in 1862 she accepted the suggestion of Great Britain that "all mail-bags clearly certified as such shall be exempt from seizure and visitation," merely adding thereto the proviso against fraud quoted on a previous page. But if Russian pride shrank from even the semblance of yielding to foreign pressure, the Russian Government might have adopted from the proposed Maritime Code of the *Institut de Droit International* the rule that a mail-boat should not be visited when an official of the Government whose flag flew over her declared in writing that she carried neither despatches nor troops for the enemy, nor contraband of war. Russia would have gained far more indirectly from the goodwill of those who benefited by such a concession than she can hope to obtain directly in the whole course of her war by standing upon the strict letter of an oppressive rule. But she went beyond her obsolete rights, and contrived most ingeniously to violate International Law in a variety of ways, when on July 15, 1904, the *Smolensk*, a cruiser of her Volunteer Fleet, stopped the German mail-packet *Prinz Heinrich* in the Red Sea, and took out of her a number of mail-bags, which she examined at leisure, and then transferred, with the exception of two, to the P. & O. steamer *Persia*, which she stopped for that purpose. To begin with, the *Smolensk* had no right to perform any acts of war at all. But, postponing this point, which we will deal with later when considering the case of the *Malacca*, we may assert with confidence that a belligerent cruiser which takes goods by force out of a neutral vessel, not because she believes them to be contraband, but in order that she may examine them to find out whether they are contraband, commits a grave offence. There is a right to capture contraband, and when it is exercised the ship which carries the unlawful goods should be brought in for adjudication with its suspicious cargo. This is the normal procedure. Some powers, however, allow the contraband goods to be taken out of the vessel, when her captain is willing to surrender them, and they are so small in quantity as to be easily carried by the capturing cruiser. But no power has ever dreamed of allowing goods to be taken from under its flag in order that a belligerent commander might do at leisure on his own ship what he ought to do on the neutral ship before he presumes to effect a seizure. No right to touch them exists till grave suspicion, if not absolute proof, arises against them. If the Russian procedure were lawful, neutral trade in time of war could be harried by a belligerent to the verge of extinction, supposing him to be at all strong at sea. He has only to stop every vessel of a power he wishes to injure, and take out as much property as he can carry for examination elsewhere, and very soon there will be nothing sent for carriage under that neutral's flag.

Further, the *Smolensk* had no business to force the *Persia* to do for it its own work of sending on the mail-bags to their proper destination. It is not a part of the duty of neutrals to fetch and carry for belligerents who have got themselves into a quandary. It is to be wished that the captain of the *Persia* had refused the task committed to him, and taken the consequences whatever they might have been. The less we, or any other neutral, concede to unauthorised Russian demands, the sooner will the present Russian attempt to force her own crude notions upon her neighbours cease, and the sooner it ceases the better for the peace of the civilised world.

Lastly, we may note that the commanders of the Russian cruisers seem to think they are at liberty to seize and confiscate any correspondence going to Japan. A more monstrous delusion never entered the head of a naval captain puffed up with national pride. The law on this matter was established during the great naval struggle which marked the end of the eighteenth and the beginning of the nineteenth centuries. It comes to this. Private correspondence goes free, but neutrals are not allowed to carry an enemy's despatches. By this phrase is meant "official communications . . . between officers, whether military or civil, in the service of the enemy on the public affairs of their Government." But even to this rule of interpretation there are exceptions. "Communications between the enemy and neutral foreign Governments," and "official communications between the enemy's home Government and the enemy's ambassador or consul resident in a neutral state," are not to be interfered with. The quotations I have given are from our own Admiralty Manual, and they form an excellent summary of the generally-accepted rules on the subject. Japan has embodied them, with a few verbal alterations, in her Prize Law. Russia, in the seventh of the "Rules" issued by the Emperor on February 28, enumerates among the acts forbidden to neutrals, "the transport of the enemy's . . . despatches and correspondence." Apparently these words are construed to cover private communications. Whether they were drawn up with that intention or not may be doubtful; but it is worthy of notice that Section 34 of the Maritime Code of the *Institut de Droit International* speaks of "correspondence officielle de l'ennemi," whereas the Russian rule, which is evidently founded on it, leaves out the qualifying adjective. If the obnoxious practice is continued, neutrals should, in self-defence, join in one emphatic protest. We thought we had advanced far on the road of tenderness to neutral interests since the violent times of the great Revolutionary and Napoleonic contests. It seems as if we had gone back instead; and it is necessary to reverse the engines before we make further progress in the wrong direction. In the special case before us, the German Government appears to have been satisfied with the reply to its remonstrance; but Mr. Balfour announced no general concession in his speech on August 25 to the deputation of ship-owners connected with the trade to the Far East.

Two of the great waterways likely to be used in connection with the present war are regulated by special treaty stipulations, and not by the common law of nations. They are the artificial passage called the Suez Canal, which connects the Mediterranean and the Red Sea, and the natural passage, called the Dardanelles and the Bosphorus, which connects the Black Sea and the Mediterranean. As complications have arisen with regard to them, we will give here a short account of the rules which apply to the transit through them of belligerent and neutral ships. If the Baltic fleet of Russia attempts the much-talked-of expedition to the Far East, a portion, if not the whole, of it will use the Suez Canal. In doing so it must observe the provisions of the Convention of 1888 for the neutralisation of the waterway. There might possibly have been some little doubt about this a few months back; for when the Convention was signed the late

Lord Salisbury, who was at that time Secretary of State for Foreign Affairs, made certain reservations as to its binding force in the then existing circumstances of the British occupation of Egypt. But any lurking suspicion that might remain has been swept away by the agreement of April 8, 1904, between France and this country. The sixth Article of the Convention referring to Egypt and Morocco contained a declaration by Great Britain of her adherence to the stipulations of 1888, "and to their enforcement. We are now, therefore, in line with the other signatory powers, and there is no excuse for a refusal on the part of any of them to consider the agreement binding. What then are its provisions as to the important matter of the passage of belligerent warships? They may pass and repass freely; but they may commit no acts of hostility in the Canal itself, or in its ports of access, or in the sea to a distance of three miles from those ports. They must not linger in the Canal, or obstruct its navigation, nor may they take in food and stores beyond what they require for present necessities. Neither troops nor material of war may be embarked or disembarked within the Canal and its ports of access. The stay of the vessels at Port Said or Suez is not to exceed twenty-four hours, except in case of distress, when permission to remain longer may be obtained. Prizes are to be subject to the same rules as the warships of belligerents. It is clear that as long as these rules are obeyed the Canal remains a neutral passage open to the vessels of all states on a footing of safety and equality. The agents in Egypt of the signatory powers are charged with the duty of watching over the execution of the Convention. In case of need they can call upon the Egyptian Government to take action for the protection of the Canal, and as Egypt would be backed up by Great Britain, the force behind the Convention is amply sufficient to secure its observance.

We will now turn to the case of the Dardanelles and the Bosphorus. It is governed by a Convention of March 30, 1856, and a Treaty signed at London on March 13, 1871. The joint effect of these two documents is to make it at once the right and the duty of Turkey, as the territorial power, to close the passage of the straits, when she is at peace, to the ships of war of all foreign states, while their merchantmen are free to pass and repass. The passage of light cruisers employed in the service of the foreign embassies at Constantinople is allowed, as also is that of the gunboats sent to guard the international works at the mouth of the Danube. And further, the Sultan has power to open the straits in time of peace to the vessels of war of friendly and allied powers, if he shall deem it necessary in order to secure the observance of the Treaty of Paris of 1856. These rules keep Russia's Black Sea fleet out of the Mediterranean, and prevent her from concentrating her naval strength. Naturally enough she submits to them with an ill grace. The Sultan she can make into a submissive instrument; but the great powers of Europe cannot be bent so easily to her will. They have signed the diplomatic documents to which we have referred, and they have no desire to see the Eastern Question raised in an acute form by an attempt to revise them or set them aside. The Black Sea fleet, therefore, has to remain in the Black Sea; but Russia habitually sends the vessels of her Volunteer Fleet through the straits under her merchant flag. These vessels belong nominally to an Association, but practically they are at the disposal of the Minister of Marine. The first three of them were bought by public subscription, raised in 1878; but since 1895 the funds of the Association have been derived chiefly from a Government subsidy of about £62,000 per annum. When the present war broke out the Volunteer Fleet consisted of fourteen cruisers and four transports. Their captains and second officers belong to the Imperial Navy. Their crews are under naval discipline, and one-third of them must consist of men who have served for five years in the Active Fleet, and have re-enlisted for two years. At all times they are in the service of the state, and act under orders received from state authorities. They are used in times of peace to take troops and criminals from Odessa and other Black Sea ports to the Far East. The tea trade and the passenger trade between these distant points are in their hands. Stores are kept for them at Vladivostock, Libau, and Odessa, the last port being their head-quarters. They habitually pass through the Dardanelles and the Bosphorus as merchantmen; but since the war began they have carried their guns and ammunition in their holds, and were thus ready to assume a warlike character at any moment.

We are now in a position to consider the case of the *Malacca*, and deal with the legal points which have arisen in connection with it. On July 4 the Russian Volunteer Fleet steamer *Peterburg* passed the Bosphorus and the Dardanelles, after having been detained by the Turkish authorities for some hours, in the course of which explanations were exchanged with the Russian ambassador at Constantinople. On July 6 she was followed by the *Smolensk*. Both flew the commercial flag. Each declared she was a merchant ship. Neither could have passed the straits in any other capacity. They maintained the same character when going through the Suez Canal. The *Peterburg* certainly, and possibly the *Smolensk* also, engaged pilots for the Red Sea as a vessel of commerce. But soon after leaving Suez she ran up the Russian naval ensign. Guns were brought out of her hold and mounted. Her armament was soon complete. She assumed the character of a warship, and proceeded to cruise against neutral commerce. On July 11, off Jeddah, she stopped and searched two British vessels, the *Menelaus* and the *Crewe Hall*; but after being detained for some time they were allowed to proceed. On July 13 she captured the Peninsula and Oriental Company's steamer *Malacca* to the north of the island of Jebel-Zukkur, and brought her to Suez on July 19. The *Malacca* was passed through the Canal in the custody of a Russian prize-crew, and flying the Russian naval flag, though, in the absence of any sentence of a Prize Court condemning her, she was still in law a British vessel. She left Port Said on July 21, her destination being unknown, but it was understood that she would be taken to Libau for trial and adjudication on a charge of carrying contraband of war.

Meanwhile there was great excitement over the case in England. The conduct of Russia was denounced with singular unanimity by the organs of public opinion. It was pointed out that the 23 tons of munitions of war carried by the *Malacca* belonged to the British Government and were destined for the dockyards of Hong-Kong and Singapore. They could not, therefore, be regarded as contraband, and there was no question of the innocence of the rest of the cargo, even when tried by the exacting Russian standard. But this, though important, was recognised as a subsidiary matter. The right of the Russian cruiser to make any captures at all was peremptorily denied and sometimes on the wrong grounds. Many newspapers declared that she was no better than a pirate; and some went so far as to demand that her prize should be rescued by force. This position was untenable in law, and had it been adopted in practice, immediate war would undoubtedly have been the result. A pirate is one who has thrown off all state authority. A pirate ship is denationalised. No Government stands behind her to be responsible for her misdeeds, and, therefore, the only way to deal with her is by direct attack. But in the case before us, however unwarrantable the acts of the *Peterburg* may have been, they were done under national authorisation. She was a Russian cruiser. Therefore Russia was responsible for her; and it was the duty of our Government to apply to the Russian Government for redress. This it did with commendable promptitude. A week after the seizure, Sir Charles Hardinge, our ambassador at St. Petersburg, handed in a strong protest against it, coupled with a demand for the immediate release of the *Malacca*. The ground taken up by our diplomacy was stated by the Prime Minister in the House of Commons on July 28 to have been "that no ship-of-war could issue from the Black Sea, and that in our judgment the members of the Volunteer Fleet, if they issued from the Black Sea and then took belligerent action, either had no right to issue or no right to take the action."

The position thus occupied by the British Government was impregnable. It raised no questions as to the exact definition of a ship-of-war and the exact formalities required to turn a merchantman into a belligerent cruiser.

Instead, attention was concentrated on the really important fact that the particular vessel whose conduct was impugned had obtained access to the waters which were the scene of her operations as a merchantman, and could have obtained it in no other way. If she were a man-of-war, her proper place was the Black Sea. If she were a vessel of commerce, she could not lawfully make captures. Assuming her to have been in reality a cruiser when she passed the straits, she could not be allowed to take advantage of her own wrong in deceiving the Turkish authorities. She must retain her simulated character, at least till the termination of the cruise which she had commenced, by writing herself down a merchantman before all the world. If she could lawfully repudiate her immediate past, and change into a ship-of-war directly she was clear of all inconvenient obstacles, what was there to prevent her from resuming her commercial character as soon as any difficulties could be surmounted by means of it? A ship cannot be allowed to masquerade about the seas as a quick-change artist. It must be either one thing or the other for some reasonable time.

No doubt a large number of states, with Great Britain among the foremost, have made arrangements with the owners of powerful steamers to take over some of the best and swiftest of their vessels in time of war, and fit them out as auxiliary cruisers. No doubt practice has been very loose as regards the methods followed in setting forth merchantmen as men-of-war, and some international agreement on the subject is highly desirable. But all this does not touch our main point in the present controversy. Russia could meet it only by asserting that she had passed ships through the straits in similar circumstances before, and had an arrangement with the Porte for doing it when she pleased. The answer to this argument is obvious. A private arrangement between two states cannot set aside the provisions of international treaties to which they are parties along with a number of other states who have neither been consulted about the agreement nor given their assent to it. The Czar's Ministers would find it hard to affirm that the arrangements with regard to the navigation of the Bosphorus and the Dardanelles concern their country and Turkey only. They would immediately be confronted with Count Schouvaloff's declaration at the Congress of Berlin in 1878, to the effect that "the principle of the closing of the straits is an European principle, and that the stipulations concluded in this respect in 1841, 1856, and 1871, confirmed at present by the Treaty of Berlin, are binding on the part of all the powers, in accordance with the spirit and letter of the existing treaties, not only as regards the Sultan, but also as regards all the powers signatory to these transactions." This pronouncement was made in answer to Lord Salisbury's statement that we did not consider our obligations went "further than an engagement with the Sultan to respect in this matter His Majesty's independent determinations in conformity with the spirit of existing treaties." The British Plenipotentiary meant, no doubt, to guard against any necessity of acquiescence in a decision of the Sultan which we had good reason to believe had been secured by threats and unscrupulous diplomatic pressure. His words certainly do not preclude us from remonstrating if the treaties are openly broken. This we did in 1903, after the passage through the straits of four Russian torpedo-boats under the commercial flag. Doubtless other cases have passed without notice. But we have never parted with the right to object, though we have not considered ourselves bound to make use of it on occasions of small importance. But the present case affects our national honour as well as our trading interests; and we can surely invoke the violated treaties, both as parties to them who have a right to see that they are observed, and as neutrals who suffer from their violation.

It is satisfactory to know that the British remonstrance was not without effect. What Mr. Balfour described as "a compromise" was reached. It was agreed that the *Malacca* should be taken to Algiers and there released after "a purely formal examination," and an assurance from the British Consul that the military stores were the property of the British Government, and the rest of the cargo was innocent. These formalities were gone through on July 27. At sunset the Russian flag, which ought never to have been hoisted, was hauled down, and at sunrise the next morning the British flag took its proper place at the mast-head. With regard to the *Peterburg* and the *Smolensk*, they "were no longer to act as cruisers," and any vessels captured by them were to be immediately released. This latter part of the agreement was carried out to the full by the liberation on July 27 of two British vessels, the *Ardova* and the *Formosa*, which had been seized in the Red Sea. No admission was made of the general principle that vessels of the Volunteer Fleet which had passed through the straits as merchantmen were legally incapable of acting as ships-of-war. Instead, it was asserted that the two steamers whose conduct was questioned had "received a special commission, the term of which has already expired"; and thus the cessation of their attacks on neutral commerce was accounted for without acceptance of the British contention.

We may admit that a compromise was necessary, while at the same time we regret some of the conditions which were agreed upon. The examination of the *Malacca* at Algiers was contrary to the fundamental principle for which we contended. The Russian Government published an official statement, on August 2, representing it as "a fresh visit." It would be hard to argue that it was nothing of the kind, though, as it took place in a neutral port, it was absolutely irregular from beginning to end. The assurance of the British Consul as to the innocence of the cargo implied that the arresting vessel had a right to inquire into the matter; whereas the head and front of our argument had been that the arrest, visit, and detention were wrongful acts, because the ship which performed them had no legal capacity to do so. In the case of the *Trent*, we demanded the release of Messrs. Slidell and Mason on the ground that it was no offence on the part of a British ship to carry them. They were set at liberty by the United States on the ground that their captor ought to have brought the ship in for adjudication instead of taking them out of her. Here was an intelligible compromise. We obtained what we wanted. The United States gave no acceptance to our legal theory. But, on the other hand, no word or act of ours gave colour to the notion that we had abandoned it.

As a result of our agreement with Russia, her two cruisers were withdrawn from the Red Sea; and on August 13 Lord Lansdowne said in the House of Lords, "We now know that instructions which have been sent to them to desist from seizures similar to those which they have previously made have reached their destination. We must therefore assume that no further seizures will take place." Unfortunately the Foreign Secretary had been misinformed, whether by accident or design it would perhaps be rude to inquire. On August 21 the *Smolensk* appeared in South African waters, and stopped the British steamer *Comedian* off the mouth of the Bashee river, which falls into the sea on the north-east coast of Cape Colony. After an examination of her papers she was allowed to proceed, and reported the occurrence next day at Durban. It was then explained from St. Petersburg that the instructions to abstain from further captures did not reach the *Smolensk* before her departure from the Red Sea, though it still remains a mystery how they contrived to miss her both at Jibuti, and at Dar-es-Salaam, the port of German East Africa where she is believed to have coaled from the *Holsatia*, a German collier chartered by the Russian Government. Count Lamsdorff, the Czar's Minister for Foreign Affairs, turned in despair to the British Government, and requested them to send the information which his own marine colleague seemed incapable of conveying. Our Admiralty issued on August 29 an announcement that they had ordered no less than seven British vessels to search for the *Smolensk*. At the time of writing (September 7) she has just been discovered off Zanzibar. It is to be hoped that now she is found she will obey the orders she receives, though they are conveyed to her by a foreign warship. Otherwise it may be necessary to terminate for a time the career of so elusive and dangerous a rover of the seas.

While England and Russia were endeavouring to come to a working agreement about the latter's auxiliary cruisers, the Turkish Government was seeking for assurances with regard to those vessels of the Russian Volunteer Fleet which still remained in the Black Sea. After some negotiation Russia consented to declare officially that they would not attempt to pass the straits loaded with arms or munitions of war, that they would retain the commercial flag during their whole voyage, and that they would not be changed into cruisers. Meanwhile we are told that a commission is sitting at St. Petersburg to inquire into the legal status of the vessels of the Volunteer Fleet. There can be little doubt that "they are properly to be considered as already belonging to the Imperial Navy" (Hall, *International Law*, 5th ed. p. 529). Their connection with the State is too close for them to be anything else but public ships. That being the case, they have no right to pass and repass the Bosphorus and the Dardanelles while the treaties of 1856 and 1871 remain in force. There may be a case for altering these instruments, but while they exist they must be observed.

It is irksome, no doubt, for the Russian Black Sea fleet to be kept out of the Mediterranean; but Russia should remember that the fleets of other powers are at the same time kept out of the Black Sea.

The application of science to warfare has been wonderfully exemplified in the present struggle, chiefly on the Japanese side. The beleaguered garrison of Port Arthur, however, appear to have utilised a marvellous invention in a clever fashion. They have installed a wireless telegraphy apparatus on one of the seaward-looking hills near the town, and from thence have got into touch with a receiving station at Chifu, seventy-seven miles away on the Chinese side of the Gulf of Pechili. They are thus enabled to communicate, in spite of the blockade, with their Government at home and their comrades in the field. The question at once arises whether the neutral power ought not to prevent the receipt of such messages on its territory. The question is a new one, but if we follow the analogy of messages sent by submarine cables there cannot be much doubt as to the answer. During the war between America and Spain in 1898 the British authorities refused a request from the United States for permission to land at Hong-Kong a cable which the American authorities proposed to lay from Manila, then in their military occupation, and to use for the purposes of their operations against Spanish territory. The refusal was based upon the ground that to grant such facilities would be a breach of neutrality. The Government of Washington acquiesced in the decision, which was given on the advice of the law officers of the Crown, and was followed by their own Attorney-General in 1899. In the course of their naval operations round Cuba they cut several cables which connected places held by the Spanish forces with neutral territory, and though after the war compensation to the extent of the actual damage suffered was voted by Congress to neutral owners, it was granted as a matter of grace and equity and not as of right. The principles underlying these incidents are twofold. The first is that belligerents have a right to prevent messages relating to the war from being sent by their enemies over means of communication which are partly in belligerent and partly in neutral territory, and to this end they may destroy neutral property at the bottom of the ocean, if there is no other means of stopping the intercourse. The second is that it is a violation of neutrality to allow facilities to one belligerent for communicating by means of neutral territory between his forces in the field and his Government at home, or his military and naval commanders in other parts of the theatre of operations. The application of this last to the case of the wireless receiving station erected by the Russians at the Chinese port of Chifu is obvious. The nature of wireless telegraphy prevents the application of the first. It was not till the end of August that the Chinese authorities awoke to the obligations of neutrality and demolished the station.

CHAPTER X

THE ALLANTON AND THE KNIGHT COMMANDER

OUR CASE AGAINST RUSSIA

THE case of the *Allanton* has not attracted so much attention as that of the *Malacca*, which it preceded in time and rivalled in importance. Public opinion was stirred to its depths in England when the news came that a vessel of the Russian Volunteer Fleet, which had just passed through the Dardanelles as a merchantman, had changed its character in the Red Sea and seized a British steamer. But the intelligence of the capture in June of one of our colliers off the coast of Japan, and her condemnation by a Prize Court sitting at Vladivostock, attracted little attention and roused no indignation. Yet a review of the circumstances will show that the security of neutral commerce is gravely compromised if the decision given in the case should be maintained. The judgment of the Russian Court is before me as I write, and I affirm deliberately that any recognition on our part of its validity would be a more serious blow to our sea-borne trade than acquiescence in the capture of a few merchantmen by unauthorised cruisers. Fortunately there is no danger of the latter calamity, and we may confidently hope that the former is equally remote.

On January 5 of the present year the *Allanton*, a British vessel registered at Glasgow, and owned by Mr. W. R. Rea of Belfast, was chartered to take a cargo of Cardiff coal to Hong-Kong or Sasebo. On February 21 she left Cardiff. At Gibraltar the captain received orders by telegraph, on February 24, to go round the Cape instead of through the Suez Canal. On May 10 he reached Hong-Kong, and there found instructions to proceed to Sasebo. Having discharged his cargo in the latter port, he went to Muroran in the island of Hokkaido, where the ship was chartered by a Japanese company to carry a fresh cargo of coal to Singapore. It was consigned to the British firm of Paterson, Simons & Co., and was part of a large quantity of 50,000 tons which they had agreed to take during the present year. The *Allanton* left Muroran on June 13, and three days later was captured by a Russian squadron near the Okishima Islands. A prize crew was put on board her, and she was taken to Vladivostock, where she arrived on June 19. After two days, and before the case was decided by the local Prize Court, the authorities commenced to discharge her cargo, a proceeding suggestive of a determination to find or make grounds for condemning her. Whether this suspicion be just or not, as a matter of fact she was condemned. The judgment of the Court was given on June 24; and four days after an appeal was lodged against it. The case is expected to come before the Admiralty Council at St. Petersburg some time in September. Meanwhile it will be advisable to examine it from the point of view of a student of International Law.

The decision of the Vladivostock Court may be divided into two main heads—that which dealt with the outward voyage from Cardiff to Sasebo, and that which dealt with the voyage from Muroran to Singapore, in the course of which the vessel was captured. Judgment was given against her in respect of both voyages. We will take them separately, and while dealing with the first we will inquire further whether considerations based upon it ought to have formed any part of the grounds of condemnation.

The Court went at length into the history of the voyage from Cardiff to Sasebo, and discovered "indisputable proof that the ship delivered recently at a Japanese port a full cargo exclusively consisting of contraband of war, with the knowledge of the owner, and with his sanction." There can be no doubt that this statement is correct. Indeed it is not disputed by the owner of the *Allanton*, and stands plainly revealed on the face of the facts as stated in a previous paragraph. But it should be noted, on the other hand, that the ship was chartered more than a month before the war broke out, and actually started on her voyage a week before coal was declared to be contraband by the Czar. If the owner had referred to "Appendix II. to § 14 of the Instructions approved by the Admiralty Council, September 20, 1900," he would have found the Russian official list of contraband goods; but he would have looked in vain for coal. The news of its inclusion arrived when his vessel was off the West Coast of Africa, and it was soon followed by the further intelligence that two British colliers, the *Frankby* and the *Ettrickdale*, which were captured in the Red Sea, had been released by order of the Czar, on the ground that they were seized before the issue of his "Rules" making coal into contraband of war (see pp. 114, 115). There was therefore every reason to believe, when the voyage began, that the Russian cruisers would regard it as perfectly innocent, and very little reason to apprehend confiscation had the vessel been captured after February 28. It is safe to say that any ordinary Prize Court would have granted indulgence in such a case, and even if it had gone the length of condemning the goods, would certainly have released the vessel. Indeed, the *Institut de Droit International* went so far as to resolve at its

Venice session in 1896 that "a carriage of contraband commenced before the declaration of war, and without necessary knowledge of its imminence, is not punishable." As a matter of fact the *Allanton* escaped capture, and delivered her cargo safely at Sasebo, a Japanese naval port.

The question now arises whether the Vladivostock Court had any right to base its condemnation of the vessel upon events which happened previous to the voyage in the course of which the seizure was made. The ordinary rule of International Law is, that the offence of carrying contraband is "deposited" as soon as the contraband goods have been delivered at their final belligerent destination. The British Admiralty Manual acts on this view, and tells our naval officers that "a vessel which carries contraband goods becomes liable to detention from the moment of quitting port with the goods on board, and continues to be so liable until she has deposited them. After depositing them, the vessel in ordinary cases ceases to be liable" (p. 23). Hall, our great English authority, says tersely and decisively, "So soon as the forbidden merchandise is deposited, the liability which is its outgrowth is deposited also" (*International Law*, 5th ed. p. 672). Professor Despagnet of Bordeaux, in his *Cours de Droit International Public*, published in 1899, writes: "Enfin, la saisie de la contrebande de guerre étant une mesure de protection de la part des Etats belligérants et non la punition d'un délit, il s'ensuit que, comme pour la violation de blocus, elle ne peut être faite que lorsque le navire va introduire la marchandise prohibée dans l'Etat ennemi; la saisie du navire est illégale quand cette introduction a eu lieu et que le navire opère son voyage de retour" (2nd ed. p. 713). A further citation of authorities may be saved by a reference to Articles 31 and 113 of the "Règlement international des prises maritimes," finally adopted by the *Institut de Droit International* at Heidelberg in 1887. They settle the matter under consideration in a few words by laying down that the contraband goods must be actually on board the vessel at the moment of search and seizure.

There can be no doubt, then, that the previous history of a vessel should not, as a general rule, influence the decision of a Prize Court upon her case. But there is in the Vladivostock judgment an obscure passage, which may indeed refer to the condemnation of the *Allanton* in respect of the voyage from Muroran to Singapore, yet seems more properly to be concerned with the decision against her on account of the voyage from Cardiff to Sasebo. Taking it as applicable to the latter, it proceeds upon the assumption that the vessel had "forfeited the rights of neutrality" on account of the conduct of its owner and its master, and was therefore subject to capture according to British practice. It then puts forward, as its own authorisation for applying so-called British rules to a British vessel, a clause in the Russian Naval Regulations, which empowers the Imperial Government to increase its severity when neutrals or enemies do not give it the benefit of rules similar to its own. If we are to judge by Russian practice in the present war, there is little chance of the contemplated case arising; and should it ever arise, the central government, and not a local court, must decide upon the measures to be adopted. But, putting this point aside, let us endeavour to extract from the judgment what, in the opinion of the Court, are the British rules which justify it in condemning a British vessel for her conduct in a voyage which had come to an end before her seizure by a Russian cruiser.

Nothing very explicit is stated; but reference is made to a passage in Sir R. Phillimore's *Commentaries upon International Law* to the effect that the vessel, as well as the cargo, can be confiscated in cases of contraband when fraud and dishonesty have been clearly proved. Undoubtedly this is a British doctrine; but it is by no means peculiar to Great Britain. The United States has adopted it; and continental jurists are divided as to its applicability. Yet, whether it is good or bad, it cannot cover the case before us. From the beginning to the end of the voyage of the *Allanton* all was open and above-board. There was no fraud and no dishonesty in any part of the whole series of transactions. All that the Russian tribunal can allege is, that the alternative destination, Hong-Kong or Sasebo, "shows that the probability of a rupture between Russia and Japan had been foreseen by the owner," and that the order to take the route round the Cape of Good Hope proves a desire to avoid the squadron of Admiral Wirenius, then cruising in the Mediterranean. Admitting both these allegations, we may ask in amazement, "Where does the fraud come in? Where is the dishonesty which is to be visited with the loss of the ship?" Here is an owner who sends his property first to a neutral and then to a belligerent destination, and takes ordinary precautions to keep it out of reach of a belligerent squadron which had just violated the neutrality of Egypt, and thus shown that it was not to be trusted. But he falsifies no papers, he keeps back no documents, he issues no instructions for the telling of a dishonest story to any cruiser who might overhaul his ship. Everything is in order on board her, and nothing is hidden. The very statements that are made against him are based upon the letters found by the searching party. The allegation of fraud is ridiculous, and the condemnation based upon it absurd.

The second attempt of the Vladivostock tribunal to find a justification for its decision in British practice is no more successful than the first. It quotes from our Admiralty Manual (p. 11) the following paragraph :—

"A person engaged in enemy navigation is also an enemy for the purposes of this chapter (*i.e.* for purposes of maritime capture), not only in respect of the particular vessel in which he is employed, but also in respect of other vessels belonging to him that have no distinct national character impressed upon them."

The Court seems to have imagined that Mr. Rea, the owner of the *Allanton*, was "engaged in enemy navigation." Apparently it never struck these astute judges that this was a strange description of a man who stayed at home during the entire voyage of the ship they were condemning, and confined his exertions as navigator to sending orders from his office for an alteration in her route and destination. If they had only glanced at the footnote at the bottom of the page before them, they would have found a reference to a case in support of the contention of the text; and on looking it up (The *Vriendschap*, 4 C. Rob. 166) they would have seen that the phrase on which they fastened described a series of actions wholly different from any which can be attributed to Mr. Rea. The owner of the *Vriendschap*, though a Dane by nationality, was "employed constantly in navigating to and from the ports of Holland," then at war with this country, and had resided in Holland for long periods, paying only "fugitive visits to the place of his birth." He was therefore deemed to have acquired an enemy character. It need hardly be said that Mr. Rea had not resided in Japan during the war, or been engaged in taking ships, whether his own or other people's, to and from Japanese ports while hostilities were going on. Yet he could not come within the meaning of the rule quoted against him unless he had done something of the kind; and even if he had done it, his present residence in the United Kingdom would protect him from the confiscation of his ship; for on the owner of the *Vriendschap* furnishing proof that he had discontinued his stay in Holland his vessel was restored to him. The excursion of the Vladivostock Court into the realm of British Admiralty procedure resulted chiefly in showing the limited nature of its equipment for the task it undertook. It might, indeed, had it been familiar with the system it refers to, have found on pages 23 and 24 of the Admiralty Manual something which at first sight seems far more suitable for its purpose. Our naval officers are there told that " If a commander meets with a vessel on her return voyage, and ascertains that on her outward voyage she carried contraband goods with simulated papers, he should detain her." Here is a sentence which definitely orders the capture of a vessel because of something which happened on a previous voyage. It would have been easy to ignore the condition as to simulated papers, and argue that, since the *Allanton* carried coals to a Japanese port a little time before she was seized in the act of carrying other coals to a neutral port, her condemnation was in accordance with British practice. Such an argument might have been plausible, though it certainly would not have been sound. An examination of the cases referred to in support of the instruction quoted above shows that the judgments turned wholly upon the facts that in the outward voyage there had been gross fraud, accompanied by perjury and the procurement of false papers, and that the return voyage was not a thing apart from the outward venture, but made along with it "one entire transaction, formed upon one original plan." It is not necessary now to discuss how far these rulings were correct at the time, or how far they would be followed by a British court to-day. Right or wrong, they form no precedents for the case of the *Allanton*, where the two voyages were entirely distinct and fraud of any kind was conspicuously absent. It may, however, be advisable to add that modern English publicists are disposed to fall into line with Continental and American authorities, and hold that there ought to be no exception to the rule that the offence of carrying contraband comes to an end with the delivery of the contraband cargo.

Having seen that there is no justification either in International Law or in British practice for the condemnation of the *Allanton* on grounds connected with her outward voyage, we are now in a position to inquire into the validity of the sentence pronounced against her in respect of the voyage in the course of which she was captured by the Vladivostock squadron. The Court acted on what it deemed cumulative evidence. It held that the course taken by the steamer on her way from Muroran was incorrect if her real destination was Singapore, that no satisfactory account was given of the presence on board of a Japanese lad, that the official Log-Book was not properly kept, and that the cargo of coal was still the property of the Japanese company which had chartered the ship. After commenting on all these matters, the judgment set forth that "A combination of all details and circumstances mentioned above, and the character of the cargo, convinces the Court that the real destination of this hostile cargo was by no means Singapore, but a Japanese or Korean port, or even the enemy's fleet manœuvring in the sea." The requisite hostile destination having thus been discovered by means of a number of inferences which implied fraud, it was but an easy step to the condemnation of the ship and cargo, which was pronounced accordingly.

Undoubtedly the cargo would have been lawful prize if it had really been destined for a port where the Japanese fleet coaled, or for Japanese men-of-war in the open sea; and in that case very possibly the ship might have been condemned as well. There would have been no difficulty about it under the Russian rule which renders neutral vessels liable to confiscation when they are found conveying to an enemy arms or ammunition in however small quantities, or other articles of contraband amounting to more than half the entire cargo (*Regulations in regard to Naval Prizes*, § 11). This severity is unauthorised by International Law unless ship and goods belong to the same owner, and neutral powers would probably have something serious to say if it were habitually enforced against them. But when the carriage of contraband is accompanied by deceit and fraud, our English practice is to confiscate ship as well as cargo; and we could not therefore have objected to the condemnation of the *Allanton,* had she been using a pretended destination and false papers to conceal the intention to convey coals to the fleet of Russia's enemy. But the inferences of the Vladivostock Court to this effect rest upon the slenderest grounds, as will be apparent when we examine the facts of the case.

As we have already seen, a hostile destination is essential in order to constitute the offence of carrying contraband. It was therefore necessary to show that the captured vessel was voyaging to a belligerent terminus. In order to do this, much was made of the fact that the *Allanton* when seized was shaping a course to the west of Japan, instead of going out into the Pacific along the east coast. From this it was inferred that she was on her way to a hostile port or a hostile fleet. But it appears that she was following the usual route taken by merchant vessels on a voyage from

Muroran to Singapore. By so doing she saved about 200 miles in distance, and from two to three days in time, the currents being much more favourable than on the alternative course. Moreover, the advantage in the matter of safe navigation lay with the route she took. The contention of her judges, that it brought her into the theatre of war, tends rather to establish her innocence than her guilt; for it stands to reason that a shipmaster who knew he was engaged in an unlawful traffic would not take his vessel into that region of sea where she was most likely to encounter cruisers who had every right to capture her. There are ample reasons why the *Allanton* should have been where she was found by the Russian squadron. So strong are they that her captain might have been accused of a grave breach of duty had he taken her elsewhere. The direction of the voyage is not only consistent with a destination to Singapore, but strongly indicates that the vessel was proceeding to that port.

It is difficult to repress a smile when reading the elaborate sentences in which the Vladivostock tribunal sets forth the arguments which led it to conclude that a Japanese lad of sixteen was in charge of a cargo of 6,500 tons of coal as agent for the Japanese company which had shipped it. Even in Japan people are not placed in responsible positions at that early age. The Court commented with perfect solemnity upon the absence of documents in his case. He had no certificate to prove his identity, no passport to give him permission to travel, and no voucher to show that he had served his time in the army or been released from military obligations. Apparently he told some story about embarking on the *Allanton* in order to go to America and complete his education. This tale is said to have been confirmed by the captain; but, as this officer neither spoke nor understood the Russian language, and complains bitterly of the disadvantage he was under during the trial owing to the absence of an interpreter, it is exceedingly likely that his statements were misunderstood. Whether that was so or not, the Court disbelieved the American story, which certainly was not very probable, if told, and very likely was not told at all. But having rejected one improbability, they immediately invented another, and magnified the Japanese lad into an important personage, rather than accept the simple explanation that he was an obscure member of the ship's company. The master and the owner both testify that he was no other, and no greater, than a cabin-boy!

Another matter which exercised the ingenuity of the Prize Court was the absence of entries in the Official Log-Book from the moment the steamer left Hong-Kong. From this it drew the inference that the ostensible destination was not the real one. The logical connection between the evidence and the conclusion is hard to find. A better explanation of the admitted fact is that, according to British law, entries are to be made in the Official Log-Book only on occasions required by the regulations of the Board of Trade. The captain asserts that no such occasion arose after the departure of the vessel from Hong-Kong. He adds, however, that in the Ship's Log, which is kept by the master for the information of the owner, entries were duly made up to the moment of capture, and full information was given as to all important matters connected with the vessel. This book showed that she was destined for Singapore, and its evidence was corroborated by the oral testimony of members of the crew, and by papers found on board, such as copies of the Charter-Party and the Bill of Lading, the Certificate of Clearance from Muroran, and a letter from the owner. No particle of written evidence was discovered which pointed to any other destination; and yet in the face of all this the judges decided "that on the second trip Singapore was no more the destination of the *Allanton* than Hong-Kong was on the first trip."

The Court concluded further that the captured cargo was enemy property. The evidence pointed the other way; for the coal was consigned to Messrs. Paterson, Simons & Co., of Singapore, who are a British firm, and goods once started on a voyage are held to be the property of the neutral consignee, if proof exists that the enemy consignor has parted with his interest in them. In this case the proof was abundant. But even if the cargo in question had been enemy property, by the second Article of the Declaration of Paris it would have been safe under the neutral flag, unless it could be regarded as contraband of war. Contraband, however, it certainly was not, provided that it was really on its way to a neutral firm in a neutral port. We are thus thrown back upon the point of destination; and those who have followed the arguments already brought forward will be at no loss as to the proper conclusion. On the one hand, there is clear and definite evidence; on the other, mere surmises. In the whole history of Prize Court procedure it would be hard to find a case where an enemy destination has been inferred on more slender grounds. Had the inference been much stronger, the facts and documents which point to the neutral port of Singapore as the real terminus of the voyage, would have sufficed to upset it. But when we find nothing better adduced in support of it than the mistake as to the vessel's course, the exaltation of a cabin-boy into an important commercial agent, and the perversion of the facts connected with the ship's papers, our surprise deepens into indignation.

There remain questions connected with the allegation of fraud and acquisition of enemy character on the part of the owner of the vessel. As before stated, it is almost impossible to tell from the text of the judgment whether its assertions on these heads, and the quotations it contained from British sources, were meant to refer to the first trip of the *Allanton* or the second. We have already dealt with them as connected with the former (see pp. 229-234); and it is only necessary to say here that the latter was equally free from fraud, and that Mr. Rea was no more "engaged in enemy navigation" on the second occasion than he was on the first. In neither case does the tribunal profit by its unfortunate attempt to invoke British authority in favour of a decision which no British Court would have dreamed of giving. There was no ground for the condemnation of the cargo. The condemnation of the ship was outrageous. We may hope that the Admiralty Council at St. Petersburg will reverse a judgment which reflects little credit upon Russian jurisprudence. In the list of members of the Council appears the honoured name of

F. de Martens, and the presence of the world-famed jurist should afford a sufficient guarantee for the observance of the law of nations. But if the highest Court of Appeal confirms the decision of the inferior tribunal, the duty of pressing for compensation and indemnity will fall upon the British Government.

We may hope and believe that our rulers will see justice done to our fellow-subjects who may suffer from the unlawful action of either belligerent. But the pretensions of the Russian tribunal in the case of the *Allanton* go beyond the infliction of grave injustice upon a British ship-owner. There is a matter at stake far more important than the wrongs of an individual. The carrying trade of the civilised world is in danger. Since the present system of maritime capture took shape, a Prize Court here and there has sometimes proved itself weak in learning and strong in bias. But the harm suffered in consequence by a few merchants and shippers has been a small thing compared with the destruction occasionally wrought on neutral trade owing to the overgrown pretensions of belligerents in matters connected with commercial policy. We shall be face to face with such an emergency if the action of the Vladivostock Court in condemning the *Allanton* for carrying coals to Sasebo is not overruled by the Court of Appeal and disavowed by the Russian Government. It will then come to a claim on the part of Russia to confiscate on the return voyage neutral vessels which carried contraband on the outward voyage. We have seen (see pp. 226, 227) that International Law gives no countenance to such a claim, and indeed emphatically repudiates it. More than a hundred years ago the greatest of British Prize Court judges endeavoured to establish one exception to the rule that the delivery of the contraband goods brings to an end all liability in respect of them. But though the decisions of Sir William Scott in the cases of the *Rosalie and Betty* and the *Nancy* were based upon clear proof of the grossest fraud in connection with the outward voyage, his ruling was never followed outside Great Britain. The courts and jurists of America repudiated it. It found no favour on the continent of Europe; and few British authorities would uphold it at the present day. Even the learned and cautious Hall says of it that "while undoubtedly severe, it does not appear to be a necessary deduction from the general principles governing the forfeiture of contraband cargoes" (*International Law*, 5th ed. p. 672). We may therefore regard the statement that the deposit of the contraband terminates the offence of carrying it as a rule without exception. If the Russian claim to disregard it is sustained, the consequences will be most serious, not only to British trade, but to the shipping of the whole world. On a rough computation, based upon the figures for 1902, out of a total Japanese import trade of about £29,000,000, cargoes to the value of fully £21,000,000 would have been liable to confiscation if the present Russian list of contraband goods is allowed to hold the field, and the present Russian determination to treat all forbidden goods as absolutely contraband is not overcome. This amounts to a practical prohibition of neutral import trade with Japan, which would be serious enough in all conscience if it stood alone. But neutral liability is doubled, when the right is assumed to confiscate on the return voyage if forbidden transport took place in connection with the outward voyage. The various claims put forth by Russia in the matter of contraband amount, when taken together, to little less than a prohibition of all sea-borne trade, export as well as import, between her enemy and neutral powers. It is impossible for an empire whose own commerce with Japan amounts to nearly a third of the whole external trade of the island realm, and which carries in addition a large portion of the goods sent and received by other countries, to sit down quietly under such an infliction. And in this connection it is comforting to notice that the interests of the United States come next in importance to our own.

Among the customs of maritime warfare, those which refer to the methods to be used by belligerent cruisers in effecting captures are not the least important. Certain rules of procedure are laid down for their guidance. They must hoist their true colours before they stop the vessel they desire to search, though they may chase under false colours. They must signal to the other ship to stop, and if ordinary signals are disregarded they may fire, first blank-guns, and finally a shot across her bows. Should these measures fail, then, and only then, has the commander of the cruiser a right to use force. If resistance is made to search, he may overcome it by arms; and the fact that it is made justifies the capture and condemnation of the vessel, even though in all other respects its voyage was perfectly innocent. Should the vessel be sunk in the process of beating down its resistance to lawful search, no offence has been committed. It has brought its fate upon itself by its unreasonable and unlawful conduct. This should be remembered in all discussions upon the various aspects of our present controversy with Russia. Neutral merchantmen have duties as well as rights, and one of them is to submit quietly to belligerent search, inconvenient and annoying though it be. On the other hand, it is the duty of belligerent cruisers, in the words of our Admiralty Manual, "to conduct the visit in a manner as little vexatious as possible." Should the examination of the papers which all merchantmen have to carry reveal any grounds of suspicion, the cargo of the visited vessel may be overhauled and an examination made of the goods on board. If this examination confirms the suspicions already excited, or raises new ones, the vessel may be detained. She is now a prize. A prize crew should be put on board, and she should be sent before a Prize Court for trial. Every maritime belligerent establishes such courts at various places in his dominions. The judges are supposed to decide upon the validity of the captures according to International Law; but they are, of course, bound to enforce any legislative acts of the state to which they belong; and if such decrees are contrary to the law of nations, the responsibility towards other states whose subjects may suffer from them rests upon the state which made them, and not on the judges which administer them. But though the law of nations provides for a judicial decision upon captures made at sea in time of war, it recognises that occasions may occur when cruisers will find it impossible to send their prizes in for adjudication. Sometimes the vessel is unseaworthy. Sometimes it is impossible to spare a prize crew. It may happen that the cruisers of the enemy swarm in the neighbourhood, or that all the accessible ports are blockaded by his fleets. In such cases destruction of prizes at sea, after providing for the safety of those on board, is recognised as a lawful though irregular proceeding, always provided that they are vessels of the enemy. This point is well illustrated by the case of the *Knight Commander*, which is so important that it will be necessary to give it in some detail.

On July 24 the Vladivostock squadron stopped the British merchant steamer *Knight Commander* about seventy miles from Yokohama. She had sailed from New York on May 6, and was carrying a mixed cargo for Yokohama and Kobe. The Russian official account says she "was chartered from America to Japan," and implies that the goods she carried were the property of American citizens. But a Reuter's telegram from Washington, dated August 9, declares that "no proof of the American ownership of a single pound of the *Knight Commander's* cargo has been produced at the State Department." The matter is important from the point of view of compensation, but not otherwise, seeing that the goods, as well as the ship which held them, were undoubtedly neutral. A hurried examination of the vessel's papers and her master convinced the Russian commander that she carried contraband of war, the bulk of her cargo being railway material and machinery. He therefore ordered her officers and crew to come on board his cruiser. When he had thus provided for the safety of human life, he sent the captured vessel and all that she contained to the bottom, the reasons assigned for this drastic treatment being "the proximity of an enemy's port, the lack of coal on board the vessel to enable her to be taken into a Russian port, and the impossibility of supplying her with coal from one of the Russian cruisers owing to the high sea running." It is doubtful whether these were sufficient in themselves to absolve the captor from the obligation to send his prize in for adjudication, even if she had been one which could lawfully be destroyed at sea in a great emergency. Yokohama was nearly a hundred miles distant. The *Knight Commander* might have been towed part of the way to Vladivostock, if her own coal was insufficient for the entire distance. There was a reasonable prospect that the weather would moderate before long, and allow the replenishing of her bunkers from those of her escort. But waiving this point, we will dwell for a moment on the question of contraband, and then go on to deal with the main issue, which is the legality or illegality of the destruction at sea of neutral vessels by belligerent cruisers.

According to the Russian Admiral Jessen, the railway material carried by the *Knight Commander* brought down upon her well-merited destruction, since it formed the bulk of her cargo, and was undoubtedly contraband of war. We may admit the fact and dispute the conclusion. Railway plant is pre-eminently one of those things which cannot be condemned or pronounced innocent on mere inspection. Accordingly it would be regarded as non-contraband by the predominant school of continental jurists, while British and American authorities would look to its probable use, as determined by its destination and other circumstances. We are not told whether the incriminated goods were destined for one of the Japanese military railways, or for the ordinary traffic of the country. Yet in the first place we should admit that they were contraband, while in the second we should deny it. Russia draws no such distinctions. As we have seen in Chapter VII., she not only sets forth a portentously long list of contraband articles, but also claims to condemn them all, if seized on their way to an enemy destination. Herein lies the sting of her present procedure. Neutrals could put up with indiscriminate confiscation, if the list of contraband was short and confined to articles of direct and immediate use in warfare. They could also put up with a long list of contraband, if a distinction was made in it between arms and munitions of war, and what is used to make them, on the one hand, and on the other articles useful indifferently for warlike and peaceful purposes, the latter being confiscated only when the surrounding circumstances showed that they were meant for the armies and navies of the enemy. Still less would neutral states have ground of complaint if the British practice were followed, and the full market price, plus 10 per cent as a fair mercantile profit, were paid to the owners of the doubtful goods. No difficulties arose in the Spanish-American war of 1898. The United States drew the British distinction between absolute and conditional contraband. Spain regarded all goods on her list as absolutely contraband; but then her list was short. It said nothing about railway plant and material, which did indeed appear in the American list, but among the goods conditionally contraband, which, we may add, is the place it occupies in the list to be found in our own Admiralty Manual. In this respect, as in so many others, Russia is following a purely retrogressive policy. She is endeavouring to reintroduce severities which have been banished from the International Code for many decades.

But, even if we assume for the sake of argument that the bulk of the cargo of the *Knight Commander* was of a highly contraband character, the case for Russia is by no means established thereby. The most important question of all remains behind. Was it a lawful act to sink the ship, instead of bringing her in for trial before a Prize Court? To this question but one answer is possible, and it is an unhesitating "No." We have already discussed the excuses put forward for the deed, and found them scarcely sufficient had the vessel sunk belonged to an enemy. But she was neutral; and International Law draws a very deep and broad distinction between the two cases. Between enemies the appeal is to force, subject of course to such limitations as the laws of war place upon its exercise. For many reasons it is desirable that the legality of all captures made at sea should be determined judicially. But if this is impossible, an enemy has no grievance when his property is destroyed, seeing that force has already decided against him and divested him of all rights in it by the fact of capture. But between a belligerent and a neutral force is not conclusive. There is always the further question whether it was lawful force, lawfully exercised. The private neutral owner is entitled to a trial, and his state is bound to see that he receives one. If it is impossible, his property should be released. His right to it remains till trial and condemnation, and when they cannot be had, the continued custody of it by the belligerent is unlawful, and its destruction an outrage. His proper course is to release it. The Maritime Code of the *Institut de Droit International* gives permission for the destruction of an enemy ship only, and before allowing such a severity insists upon the existence of emergencies greater than those which in the opinion of Admiral Jessen justified the sinking of a neutral prize (*Tableau General*, pp. 205, 206). Great Britain in her Admiralty Manual (p. 86) definitely orders the release of a neutral ship if she is unseaworthy, or if a prize crew cannot be spared to navigate her. The Prize Law of Japan, as given in Appendix VII. of

Professor Takahashi's excellent book, *International Law during the Chino-Japanese War*, contains a similar provision.

In following the opposite course Russia runs counter to the opinion of the civilised world. Section 21 of her *Regulations in regard to Naval Prizes,* adopted in 1895, and Section 40 of her *Instructions* to her naval officers, issued in 1900, describe the circumstances in which captured vessels may be burnt or sunk, without any hint at a distinction between the vessel of a neutral and the vessel of an enemy. Her officers were but obeying their own orders when they destroyed the *Knight Commander*; but nevertheless they were committing a gross breach of International Law, for which we must hold their Government responsible. A great commercial nation like England cannot for one moment admit that her merchantmen may be sent to the bottom, innocent or guilty, whenever the commander of a belligerent cruiser, acting on strange notions as to contraband, finds it inconvenient to spare a prize crew. In far rougher times than the present her courts have given damages to neutrals whose ships were destroyed by her cruisers. The greatest of her Prize Court judges declared that such destruction could only be justified to the neutral, even when it was of the gravest importance to the captor's own State, "by a full restitution in value"; and one of the greatest of her publicists wrote a few years ago that "to destroy a neutral ship is a punishable wrong; if it cannot be brought in for adjudication it can and ought to be released" (Hall, *International Law*, 5th ed. p. 735). The precedents adduced in Russia's favour are no precedents at all. Those who have brought them forward betray a curious incapacity to see the point of the case against her. It is not that she destroyed prizes at sea, but that she destroyed a neutral prize. The confederate cruiser, *Alabama*, did undoubtedly burn and sink during the American Civil War a number of merchantmen she had captured; but they were all Federal merchantmen, and her justification lay in the fact that she could not take them into a Southern port owing to the strictness of the Northern blockade. The supposed parallel breaks down utterly. It is satisfactory to learn on the authority of the Secretary of State for Foreign Affairs that "the language of the Russian Government justifies us in hoping that these acts of destruction of neutral prizes are not likely to be repeated" (Speech in House of Lords, August 11). It will be still more satisfactory to know that this assurance is general in terms, and that full compensation has been paid both for the ship unlawfully destroyed and the cargo sent to the bottom without sufficient proof that it was really contraband of war.

The fate of the *Knight Commander* is not the only instance of the destruction of neutral merchantmen. There are two others. On July 16 the British steamer *Hipsang* was fired upon in Pigeon Bay not far from Port Arthur. Eventually she was struck by a torpedo fired from a Russian destroyer. The greater part of her crew were rescued, but some were wounded and others drowned. There is a direct conflict of evidence with regard to the conduct and treatment of the vessel. The Russian captain declares that she obstinately refused to stop, and fired back at the destroyer. The English captain affirms that he hoisted his flag and stopped his engines directly he heard a shot. It is impossible to decide between assertion and assertion; but it may be noted that a Naval Court held at Shanghai on August 22 decided without reserve that the steamer behaved correctly. If this be true, the attack on her, with the consequent loss of human life, was a wanton outrage, far worse than the sinking of the *Knight Commander.* On the other hand, if the Russian account proves to be correct, the obstinate refusal of the *Hipsang* to submit to lawful search, and her futile attempt at resistance, amply justify the force used against her, and absolve those who used it from blame for the result. A similar conflict of testimony has occurred in the case of the German vessel *Thea,* which was captured by the Vladivostock squadron on July 26. She was navigated by a Japanese crew, carried a cargo of fish, and is said to have been engaged in the Japanese coasting trade, and to have enjoyed all the privileges accorded to Japanese merchantmen. This last allegation is denied in

Berlin; while it is admitted that she had availed herself of the provisions of a Japanese decree, dated February 2, 1904, opening the coasting trade to ships of all nations. No opinion of any value can be formed without further evidence. It may be that she was justly regarded by the Vladivostock Prize Court as having been incorporated in enemy commerce and subject to enemy control, in which case her neutral character would undoubtedly have been forfeited, and she would have acquired the disabilities of an enemy vessel, including the liability to be sunk if she could not be taken in for adjudication. But when we remember the previous exploits of the tribunal in question, we shall hardly be likely to fall into the error of attributing too much importance to its decision.

It may be doubted whether the nation understands the vast importance of the questions discussed in the preceding pages. On each separate matter as it arose public opinion was strongly excited, sometimes to an undue extent. But the cumulative effect of all the Russian pretensions taken together has not as yet been realised. Unless they are withdrawn or curbed other maritime nations will put forth similar claims; and we, as the greatest of the trading peoples, shall be the chief sufferers. When we are neutral, the extended list of contraband, and the arbitrary increase in the penalties for carrying it, will cripple our external commerce. When we are belligerent, the enemy, if he can place a few cruisers on the ocean, will intercept our supplies of food and raw material, even when carried in neutral vessels to purely commercial ports. A war of starvation will be waged against the power whose navy is too strong to be overcome in open battle. Not only is our own security menaced, but the welfare of the civilised world also. Instead of advance we see everywhere retrogression—days of grace shortened, the right of search used to the fullest extent without regard for the interests and susceptibilities of neutrals, no immunities granted to mail-steamers, the law of contraband so extended that nearly all trade with the enemy is brought within it, and that at a time when the blockade of one of the least of his ports is utterly out of the question, the penalties on neutral vessels engaged in forbidden acts arbitrarily increased, till few can feel secure against destruction at sea without trial and without redress, neutral sovereignty flouted wherever it can be done with impunity, protests disregarded, concessions evaded, and pledges broken. And now, as if all this were not enough, comes the alleged attempt to differentiate against Great Britain in the treatment accorded to neutrals. The facts are disputed; and the shipping statistics of the whole Eastern trade will not enlighten us. It is the external commerce of Japan which is in question; and in 1902, of the non-Japanese ships engaged in it 1639 were British, and 1298 belonged to other nations, 382 being German. We should, therefore, expect British and German ships to be stopped in the ratio of rather more than 4 to 1, whereas the actual proportion is nearly 8 to 1. But the mere numbers count for little or nothing. What is much more significant is the difference of treatment and the difference of insurance rates. According to the information received up to mid-September the German steamer *Arabia* and part of her cargo were released by the Vladivostock Prize Court, the flour and railway material she carried being condemned, while the British steamer *Calchas* was detained for some weeks longer before a more severe judgment was passed upon her. It was said on August 13 that war risks on cargo shipped for Japan in German vessels were insured at 5s. per cent, while similar cargoes in British vessels were charged from 20s. to 40s. per cent. Possibly further knowledge may necessitate a modification of some of these statements; but there seems to be no doubt about it that all through August British shipping companies were refusing to carry goods to Japan, while their German rivals were eagerly taking all that was offered, and increasing their services to meet the demand. Our ship-owners are a singularly clear-headed and enterprising race of men; and though they may have been the victims of panic, they are the last persons we should suspect of anything of the kind.

Let us look at the matter in the light of our knowledge of ordinary human nature. On the one hand, we have the effusive sympathy with Russia expressed by the German Emperor, and the palpable neglect of the German Government to enforce its neutral obligations, and stop the original departure from its ports of the swift cruisers bought in Germany by Russia, and now fitted out as vessels of war to interfere with neutral commerce. Add to this that in the remonstrances about the seizures of the *Prinz Heinrich* the inconvenient question of the status of the Volunteer Fleet was not raised. On the other hand, it is notorious that British sympathies are almost entirely on the side of Japan, and that public opinion in Russia has been, and to some extent still is, stirred up against us as allies of Russia's enemy, and responsible (so it is said) for the outbreak of the war. What more natural than that everything German should be treated with indulgence, and everything British with severity! We need not suppose there is any express agreement to that effect. Such matters are not reduced to writing. A hint and a shrug of the shoulders are all that is required, and the thing is done.

Our Government should watch carefully, and with no preconceived idea that the charge of preference for Germany must be mistaken. If they find that discrimination is used against us, then it will be one of their chief duties, as Mr. Balfour said to the ship-owners' deputation on August 25, "to see that absolute equality of treatment was meted out to British shipping as compared with foreign shipping." The knowledge that we are determined and alert will probably be enough to check any tendency in the opposite direction. Belligerents are bound to treat neutrals alike, just as neutrals are bound to treat belligerents alike. Sympathies may be what they will; but actions must be impartial. To the right of search we must submit, even though we may be convinced that the conditions of modern commerce and modern warfare will before long necessitate its modification. But we may demand that it shall be exercised without favour, and with as little annoyance as possible to neutral trade. Russia seems at last to be awaking to the fact that behind the courteous wording of our remonstrances lies a determination to see that they are effective. She has agreed that no neutral trading ships shall in future be sunk by her men-of-war, and that vessels of her Volunteer Fleet which have passed the Bosphorus and Dardanelles as merchantmen shall not be used as cruisers. She has also appointed a commission to study the question of contraband; and in the matter of food and coal it has decided in favour of the views set forth by our Government and the Government of the United States in the protests which we rejoice to find they have made on common grounds. There are other questions, such as the restriction of the area of search and the concession of immunities to mail-steamers, on which Russia might gracefully yield to the public opinion of the civilised world. But where we have put forward demands as of undoubted right, she must understand that there is but one alternative to granting them. The nation stands solid behind its rulers in the determination to have its food supplies freed from the menace of destruction, its trade secured from new and barbarous penalties, and the honour of its flag upheld.

CHAPTER XI

DID JAPAN VIOLATE KOREAN NEUTRALITY? THE POSITION IN INTERNATIONAL LAW OF KOREA AND MANCHURIA. THE CASE OF THE RESHITELNI

In the present war, as far as it has gone, fighting has taken place on the high seas, in the territorial waters of the belligerents, in the Liautung peninsula, in the empire of Korea, and in the province of Manchuria. Little need be said about the first two. In the discussion as to marine mines we dealt with their use for warlike purposes, and saw that the project of an extension of territorial waters beyond their present somewhat narrow limits derived additional force from a consideration of the mining and countermining operations of belligerent squadrons. We may point out here that supermarine as well as submarine methods of warfare enforce the same lesson. With the marine league as the ordinary distance and the ten-mile rule for bays and estuaries, it is quite possible, owing to the enormous range of modern artillery, that a great naval battle may be fought on the high seas, and yet shipping in some neutral port, or life and property on neutral land, may be seriously injured by stray projectiles. It is true that the question of the advisability of extension does not turn on these considerations alone. We do not profess to discuss it here, but merely to point out that the increase in the effectiveness of armament is an important factor in the problem. With the remark that, though differences of opinion exist as to the proper extent of territorial waters, no one doubts that those of the belligerent powers, as well as the high seas, are lawful battle-ground, we pass on to the consideration of the Liau-tung peninsula as a portion of the field of hostilities.

What is the Liau-tung peninsula? For our present purpose we shall define it as that territory which was made over to Russia by

China in 1898, and in the following year erected into the province of Kwang-tung by a Russian Imperial Ukase. The first Article of the agreement of transfer runs thus:

"The Emperor of China agrees to lease to Russia Port Arthur and Ta-lien-wan, together with the adjacent seas, but on the understanding that such lease shall not prejudice China's sovereignty over this territory."

The lease was to subsist for twenty-five years, with power of extension by common accord. It included not only the two places named, but a considerable district to the north-east of them. The powers conveyed by it are spoken of as those of "usufruct" in the official communication to the Russian press. Now, in Roman law usufruct was the right of using and reaping the fruits of things belonging to others, without destroying their substance. As to a lease, we are familiar in our own law with the powers of lessor and lessee. The matter is simple enough when such things as a house or a flock of sheep are concerned. But how does it work out when we have to deal with state authority? Who has jurisdiction in a leased territory, the state which grants the lease or the state to which the lease is granted? Or have they concurrent authority therein? If jurisdiction belongs to the grantor state, what are the rights which have been transferred to the grantee by the lease? If the grantee can exercise jurisdiction, what rights remain to the grantor whose sovereignty is supposed to be unimpaired? If both states share jurisdiction, where is the boundary line to be drawn between their respective spheres? There is no limit to the legal conundrums that might be invented by a little ingenuity. But in order to solve them satisfactorily we must qualify the theories of jurists by considerations drawn from the hard facts of international intercourse. And, after all, old theories which fail to explain new facts are themselves in need of modification. Law was made for men and states, not men and states for law.

Turning then to facts, we note an agreement of opinion among all the powers except Japan, that when once Russia had obtained a lease of

Port Arthur, Germany of Kiao-chau, and Great Britain of Wei-hai-Wei, foreign consuls in those places could no longer exercise the special powers granted to them by treaty with China. The territories in question were held to be under the full and exclusive jurisdiction of the states to which they were leased, whose authority was deemed supreme while the leases remained in operation. Further, we must remember that the administration passed entirely to the lessee states, who not only carried on the government, but erected fortifications, established garrisons, and even dealt with the Chinese inhabitants as resident aliens. Bearing these things in mind, we are forced to the conclusion that a lease in international transactions is not the commonplace and innocent affair we know so well in dealings with private property. It amounts, in fact, to a cession of the leased territory for a limited time, and with a strong probability that the period mentioned in the lease will be prolonged indefinitely if the lessee-state finds it convenient to stay on. With regard to it, law and fact harmonise but badly, and the difficulty arises from the useful diplomatic habit of veiling harsh acts with pleasant terms. The words which reserve the sovereignty of the lessor are fine phrases used for the purpose of disguising the reality of territorial transfer. They may be likened to the jam which renders palatable the child's powder, or the courteous formula which conceals a social rebuff. We regret our inability to accept the invitation we regard as an impertinence. We are the obedient servants of the letter-writer we wish to keep at arm's-length. In the society of nations there are similar forms, and the lease is one of them. As a rule words describe things. In diplomacy they are sometimes used to describe—well, other things!

If we apply these considerations to the position of Russia at Port Arthur and Ta-lien-wan, otherwise Dalny, we see at once that the powers she exercised there, from the moment they came into her possession six years ago to the outbreak of the present war, were powers of sovereignty and nothing else. She held dominion over the whole district; and accordingly when hostilities began she used it without limit or restraint for warlike purposes, and was subject in it to the onset of her foe. It is worthy of remark that, though she denounced Japan's first attempt on Port Arthur as treacherous, she never maintained that the place, and the leased territory generally, were free from attack, as being under the sovereignty of China and therefore neutral ground. There can be no doubt that the whole world looks upon Port Arthur and Dalny as Russian territory; and unless the whole world is wrong, Russia was right in filling the district and its waters with troops and warships, and Japan was right in doing her utmost to destroy or capture them.

The next matter for discussion is the legal position of Korea in relation to the war. It is curious and anomalous in no small degree. We cannot even begin to understand it without glancing back at the previous history of the country. It has already (see p. 9) been pointed out that by the Treaty of Shimonoseki, which in 1895 ended the war between China and Japan, the former power was made to recognise "the full and complete independence and autonomy of Korea." Taking this as our starting-point, we go on to another important diplomatic document, the famous Treaty of Alliance for five years between Great Britain and Japan which was signed in 1902. Not only does it set forth the limited nature and purpose of the alliance, but it also gives the reasons which led the high contracting parties to become allies. They felt themselves to be specially interested in maintaining the independence and territorial integrity of China and Korea, and in securing equal opportunities therein for the commerce and industry of all nations. Having these ends in view, they "mutually recognise the independence" of the two states, and "declare themselves to be entirely uninfluenced by any aggressive tendency in either country." So far all is noble. We seem to be reading a generous guarantee of free and unfettered national existence to two self-respecting and patriotic states. But the vision of the allies as fairy godmother to a pair of beauteous but persecuted international Cinderellas vanishes at the next sentences of the first Article of the treaty. We are back again in the world of the selfish and the commonplace when we read:—

"Having in view, however, their special interests, of which those of Great Britain relate principally to China, while Japan, in addition to the interests she possesses in China, is interested in a peculiar degree politically, as well as commercially and industrially, in Korea, the High Contracting Parties recognise that it will be admissible for either of them to take such measures as may be indispensable in order to safeguard those interests if threatened either by the aggressive action of any other Power, or by disturbances arising in China or Korea, and necessitating the intervention of either of the High Contracting Parties for the protection of the lives and property of its subjects."

So, after all, the allies have a care for their own interests, and the independence of China and Korea is conditioned thereby! If the proceedings of other powers endanger these interests, the cry of "Hands off" may be raised against them. If local disturbances arise, either of the High Contracting Powers may intervene to protect its subjects. Then follow stipulations for mutual aid in case either of the allied states should be involved in war with more than one power, in defence of the interests just described. Clearly the independence recognised in the treaty is of a peculiar kind. The intervention of the allies is not held to be inconsistent with it. They may take what measures they please, without regard to the wishes of the Chinese or Korean Governments, to foil the aggressions of other powers or put down local disturbances. Have we not here another example of the diplomatic use of words in non-natural senses?

It is impossible to blame either Great Britain or Japan. Our stake in the commerce of China and the Far East is so enormous that we have ample justification for strong measures against the policy of grab and exclusion which finds favour with some of our neighbours. They are constantly putting pressure to bear on China against us, and we must of course reserve the right to put on counter-pressure, while equally of course we must disclaim any interference with so sacred a thing as national independence. Japan's interest in preventing the preponderance of Chinese or Russian influence in Korea is vital. If we bear in mind all these things we shall look upon the stipulations of the treaty as reasonable, while at the same time we recognise that its wording on the subject of the independence of Korea gives colour to the charge made against Japan of violating, when it suited her own purpose, the rights she was so anxious to safeguard against other powers. Technically there is some ground for the accusation. Practically Korea never has been, and was never meant to be, fully independent in the sense given to the term by international jurists. Russia, while using against the proceedings of the Japanese Government arguments based upon the constant verbal recognition of Korean independence, did not scruple to put every pressure short of actual war upon the Court of Seoul. There was a diplomatic duel between her and Japan on Korean soil from 1895 to 1904, when the conflict of arms succeeded the conflict of arts. It was a fight for permanent and preponderating influence, and whichever side got the better of it for the moment, Korea was never really independent. As war became imminent the Emperor and his Court fell into a condition of ludicrous distress. They loved neither side, and dared not offend either. In their perplexity they proclaimed the neutrality of Korea in January, though they had no means of making it effective should the anticipated war break out. A small force of Japanese infantry was in the capital, and Cossack patrols paid scant respect to the integrity of the northern frontier. It was clear that, if war came, the country would be the scene of belligerent operations, and power over it the prize of the victor.

Things were in this condition when on February 8 the squadron of Admiral Uriu steamed into the harbour of Chemulpo and commenced to disembark Japanese troops. Early the next morning the Admiral requested the captain of the Russian cruiser *Variag* to leave the harbour, and informed him that, if he did not, he would be attacked. Thereupon the commanding officers of the British cruiser *Talbot*, the French

Pascal, and the Italian *Elba* made the joint protest we have already discussed (see pp. 76-78).

As we have seen, the protest was hardly called for, even if a violation of neutrality had been in progress. We have now to consider whether what was done amounted to anything of the kind. Was the action of Japan a breach of International Law? Russia has exhausted the language of denunciation with regard to it. In Count Lamsdorff's circular note of February 22 he speaks of it as "a dastardly attack," and accuses the Japanese Government of acting "in spite of all treaties, in spite of its obligations, and in violation of the fundamental rules of International Law." Japan has replied in a much calmer document published early in March. She maintains that her troops were sent to Korea with the consent of the Korean Government, and for the purpose of maintaining the independence and territorial integrity of the country against the machinations of Russia. A state of war, so she contends, existed when the two Russian vessels were attacked by her squadron; and "Korea having consented to the landing of Japanese troops at Chemulpo, that harbour had already ceased to be a neutral port, at least as between the belligerents."

There is an air of unreality about the whole controversy. Both sides find it convenient to keep up the diplomatic fiction that Korea was, or could be, an independent state. If she were, clearly her neutrality ought to have been respected, but no less clearly ought she to have been free from Russia's attempt to prevent her from throwing Yongampo open to foreign trade, and even to occupy it under cover of her own timber concession on the Yalu. It is a curious doctrine that the consent of a state to the landing of the troops of one belligerent in a port deprives that port of its neutral character as between the belligerents, but not otherwise, while apparently it has no effect upon the status of the rest of its territory. The truth is that here we have another instance of that divorce between hard facts and diplomatic phrases which we have discovered so frequently, as we traced the course of the present troubles in the Far East. The neutrality of Korea is as much a mere phrase as its independence. A territory cannot be neutral when war is being waged in it, and for it. In an armed struggle facts count, and phrases divorced from facts go to the wall. Having for years intrigued and negotiated for Korea without agreement and without decisive effect, Japan and Russia began to fight for her. There was war for Korea and in Korea, if not with Korea. The power which struck the first blow within Korean borders violated no neutrality existing in actual fact, though a state-paper neutrality was rudely interfered with.

Japan took the earliest opportunity of regularising her position in Korea by a Protocol negotiated with the native Government, and communicated from Tokio to her legations abroad on February 27. In this, the last of the long series of diplomatic agreements relating to the subject, the fiction of Korean independence is still kept up, while the fact of Japanese control is further accentuated. By the third Article Japan "guarantees the independence and territorial integrity of the Korean Empire"; and by the second she covenants to "ensure the safety and repose of the Imperial Household of Korea." The Korean Government, on its part, covenants to adopt the advice of Japan "in regard to improvement in administration," and to give full facilities for the promotion of any measures the Japanese Government may undertake to protect Korea against foreign aggressions or internal disturbances. It also agrees that for the promotion of these objects Japan may occupy strategic points on Korean territory.

The effect of this agreement has been to place the resources of Korea at the disposal of Japan in the present war. The victorious army which forced the passage of the Yalu so brilliantly on May 1 was landed at Korean ports, concentrated on Korean soil, and supplied from Korean harbours. In the political sphere Korea has denounced, as having been made under compulsion, all her treaties with Russia and all concessions granted to Russian subjects. On the other hand, Russia has declared that she will regard as null and void all the acts of the

Korean Government while under Japanese tutelage, and her newspapers loudly proclaim that, if our neutrality were genuine, we should raise objections against the Protocol, as being inconsistent with the Treaty of 1902, whereby we, in conjunction with Japan, mutually recognise the independence of Korea. In reality there is no inconsistency, because, as we have just seen, it is clear from the first Article of the Treaty that the independence in question was not an ordinary independence, but a diplomatic variety which was perfectly consistent with recurring interventions to ward off foreign aggression and put down domestic revolt. In other words, it was a dependent independence, or no independence at all, and such it remains under the agreement of February 1904. That instrument undoubtedly establishes a Japanese Protectorate over Korea, and the beauty of Protectorates is their indefiniteness. As Professor Nys, the great Belgian jurist, says in his recently published work on *Le Droit International*, "Le terme 'protectorat' désigne la situation créée par le traité de protection. . . . Le protectorat a plus ou moins de développement; rien n'est fixé dans la théorie; il est cependant un trait caractéristique commun aux États protégés c'est qu'ils ne sont pas entièrement indépendants dans leurs relations avec les autres États" (vol. i. p. 364). These words exactly fit the condition of Korea under its recent agreement with Japan. Indeed, the description might be extended to its internal affairs also. Susceptibilities are soothed, and possibly diplomatic difficulties turned, by calling it independent; but in reality it is as much under Japanese protection as Egypt is under ours, all state-paper descriptions to the contrary notwithstanding. The new treaty of August 22, 1904, shows that this is fully recognised at Tokio. A financial adviser and a diplomatic adviser are to be appointed by the Korean Government on the recommendation of Japan, and nothing important is to be done in their departments without their advice. No treaties with foreign powers are to be concluded, and no concessions to foreigners granted, without previous consultation with the Japanese Government.

We must now endeavour to establish the legal status of the great province of Manchuria in view of the present war. Fortunately the question, though by no means free from complications, is simple by comparison with that of Korea. Two facts are undeniable, and those two facts rule the situation. The first is that Manchuria is still in law a portion of the Chinese Empire. The second is that the troops of Russia hold the greater part of it, and within that part her officers exercise full authority. Now there is no part of the international law of war more clear, and none more generally accepted, than the principle that when the armed forces of a state hold a territory not her own in firm possession, so that they can exercise their authority at will in any part of it, they possess over that territory and its inhabitants certain wide rights, called the rights of occupancy, and these rights remain as long as the fact of presence and control on which they are based remains. They apply to any foreign territory firmly held for warlike purposes, no matter how the tenure originated. It may be territory of the other belligerent won in fair fight. It may be territory of a neutral obtained by means which will not bear investigation. The question of how it was acquired is not relevant. The only thing that really matters is the fact of firm possession.

No one denies that the outbreak of the war found Russia in full control of all but the south-western portion of Manchuria, but few recognise the importance of the legal consequences that follow. The occupant can demand certain services from the inhabitants of the occupied territory. He can levy therein forced supplies, called requisitions, of food and other things necessary for the daily needs of his army, and these requisitions fall on the property of neutral subjects within the zone of occupation, as well as on the property of subjects of the enemy. He can punish with death any attempt on the part of the inhabitants to join his foes, or to destroy his lines of communication, or to cut off his stragglers, or even to give information of his movements. He is indeed bound to protect those who follow their peaceful avocations, and to keep his troops from indiscriminate outrage and plunder. But he may strip a district of corn and cattle by means of his requisitions, and he may tear men away from their farms or their factories to drive his teams, guide his marching columns, carry his wounded, or act as artificers for his engineers and artillery. The Proclamation of Admiral Alexeieff to the people of Manchuria, on February 24, was couched in terms of unnecessary severity; but in substance most of it did not go far, if at all, beyond Russia's rights as military occupant, though the threat to hold responsible all the officials and people of districts where the railway line and telegraph wires were cut came strangely from a nation which regarded our much milder proceedings in the Boer War with indignation and horror. No justification can, however, be found for the statement at the end that "if officials or people treat with enmity the Russian army, the Russian Government will assuredly exterminate these persons, showing no mercy." This is either wolfish cruelty or mere bombast, and reflects nothing but discredit on the high official who is responsible for it. But he gave prominence to the best side of the international code when he bade all the inhabitants of Manchuria continue their usual avocations, and added, "When Russian troops enter your neighbourhood you should treat them with confidence, and in return the Russian troops will not ill-treat you, but will accord you extra protection." Nor did he contravene accepted rules when he ordered the people to give information of the whereabouts of "the Chunchuses, the red-bearded brigands who are the curse of Manchuria," and declared that "any one secretly harbouring them would be punished as if he were one himself." Every army must protect itself from the attacks of irregular bands, half-criminals, half-patriots. War is horrible, even when it is conducted with humanity. It cannot be made with kid gloves and rose-water.

There can be no doubt that whenever a power at war exercises full military control outside her own territories, then she can enforce the rights of belligerent occupation. Russia acted on this principle when she proclaimed martial law at

Niu-chwang at the end of last March, and interfered in a most drastic manner with neutral trade at that port, in order to carry out measures of precaution in view of an expected Japanese attack. Commerce suffered severely, but no ground was given for international complaint, apart from some acts of unnecessary harshness in details. The rights of western traders at Treaty Ports in the Chinese Empire cannot override the exigencies of warfare. But as soon as the military necessity for interfering with them has passed away, they will revive, unless further stipulations are made meanwhile with regard to them. Japan proclaims her intention of handing back to China those portions of Manchurian territory which she delivers by force of arms from the grip of Russia. If and when China receives them back, she will take them with their legal obligations. These last have been suspended by the military occupant for his own purposes, but the normal state of affairs is restored as soon as his occupation ceases. While it remains, however, the usual results follow. It is beside the mark to say that Russia ought not to be in possession. She is there, and from that fact flow legal consequences which cannot be ignored.

We may apply the same reasoning to those districts in South-western Manchuria which Russia evacuated under the Convention of 1902, and has reoccupied during the present war. Doubtless this reoccupation was a wrongful act. Had China been a strong neutral she would have prevented it, as she had every right to do. But she attempted nothing of the kind. Russia is there again; and from that it follows that she can deal with the places in question as occupied territory, and Japan can attack them, if she pleases, without laying herself open to the charge of infringing Chinese neutrality.

This question of Chinese neutrality will in all probability lead to curious developments. Japan is growing restive under the provocation of seeing Russia first reoccupy and obtain supplies from towns and districts which were not in her military possession when the war broke out, and then, when forced to evacuate them, endeavour to get China to hold them and keep out Japanese troops. Her patience seemed to come quite to an end when a number of Russian ships took refuge in various neutral ports after the great sea-fight off Port Arthur on August 10. Among these was the destroyer *Reshitelni*, which entered the harbour of Chifu about midnight, and lay there for twenty-seven hours, till she was seized and towed away by two Japanese destroyers about 3 A.M. on August 12. During the time she spent in port, negotiations were carried on between her commander and the Chinese authorities, and there is a direct conflict of testimony as to their result. The Russian captain says, "I disarmed the ship and lowered my flag"; and Admiral Alexeieff declares that the breech blocks of the guns and rifles were handed over to the Chinese Admiral. On the other hand, the Japanese captain Fujimoto reported that his officer "found the *Reshitelni* still not disarmed"; and the justificatory statement issued by the Japanese Government states without qualification that "the vessel was fully armed and manned when visited by Lieutenant Terashima in the early morning of the 13th instant." But even if we accept the Japanese account as accurate in every particular, we are nevertheless forced to the conclusion that a gross breach of neutrality was committed. The occurrence reflects no credit upon a power which up to that time had been careful to keep its conduct correct according to the standards of International Law. The assertion that the entry into a Chinese port of a fugitive Russian destroyer constituted an occupation of that port for warlike purposes, and justified a disregard of its neutrality by Japan, will not bear a moment's examination. A hunted refugee is not a military occupant. The further argument that the *Reshitelni* was the aggressor, because her captain struck with his fist the Japanese officer who came on board with an armed party and ordered him to surrender his ship, reminds one irresistibly of the fable of the wolf and the lamb. Special pleading of this kind injures rather than helps the case of those who resort to it. And there is a case for Japan, not indeed as regards the sudden and violent seizure of the *Reshitelni*, but on the general question of the failure of China to enforce her commands upon the shattered Russian warships which entered her waters. The record of the orders and counter-orders, the vacillations and defiances, connected with the *Askold* and the *Grosovoi* at Shanghai, is at once pitiful and ludicrous. Japan does well to remember how the *Mandjur* stayed, still armed, in the same port for weeks after receiving notice to quit, how the Russian wireless telegraphy station was installed at Chifu, and how Russian troops took supplies from parts of Manchuria supposed to be outside the zone of warlike operations. She cannot be expected to split up her naval strength into small squadrons after a successful engagement, and use them to watch her crippled opponents waiting in Chinese harbours for the possible advent of the Baltic fleet. She did well to give notice that, unless a real and complete disarmament were effected, she would do her own police-work inside Chinese waters as well as on the high seas. But she did ill to take matters into her own hands at Chifu, suddenly and without warning, before there was time to see whether the obligations of neutrality were properly performed.

Russia has endeavoured to secure the retirement within the Great Wall of China's one small army of drilled and disciplined troops, and has protested against the presence with them of Japanese instructors. On these points her legal case is bad, though the military and political reasons for her anxiety are very obvious. Surely a neutral state can distribute its troops as it pleases within its own territory, and hire what persons it pleases to teach them their craft. But the most serious symptom of all is the expressed determination of Russia to hold China responsible for the action of the Chunchuses and other irregulars, whose activity seems to increase with every Japanese success, and who are becoming a serious danger to General Kuropatkin's communications. She is but reaping as she sowed. The cruelties which accompanied the restoration of order in Manchuria in 1900, and the plunderings and severities that have been common since the present war began, have naturally raised against her the anger of a population which remembers well the admirable conduct of the Japanese armies when they occupied parts of the same province in 1894 and 1895. She is bound to deal with her own difficulties, and has no sort of right to throw them upon another power on the plea that the state in question is not only neutral but also sovereign in Manchuria. China is both; but Russia has the territory under her military occupation, and is therefore bound to police it. She must not deprive her eastern neighbour of all power over vast districts, and then call upon her to exercise authority within them. Where she claims the rights of a military occupant she must perform his duties also, or be content to suffer from the lack of performance. She cannot eat her cake and have it too.

INDEX

THE END

Printed by R. & R. Clark, Limited, *Edinburgh*

Made in the USA
Monee, IL
04 November 2026

67384990R00177